The secrets we keep

By: Faye Valentine

WARNING: This book contains sexual assault, child abuse, domestic violence, Suicide, Self-harm, addiction, and animal abuse. It was exhausting both mentally and physically to relive some of my most traumatic life moments and put them into words. I hope to bring understanding and awareness to many subjects. I have changed names and places in order to protect their identity. A courtesy I was never privileged with. I hope you enjoy my life story.

Index

Chapter 1
Motherhood.

Everyone has things they would never tell anyone. Secrets you'd rather die than tell. For the first 18 years of my life everything was a secret. My mom Michelle was an "accident." Michelle's mom Laurie cheated on her husband and got pregnant. Keeping Michelle meant the end of her marriage. Laurie's brother Rice and his wife Pauline couldn't have kids. They tried and tried but never had any luck. Laurie gave Michelle to Rice and Pauline who adopted her from birth. They adored her. Rice was a Vietnam veteran and a Christian preacher. He used the bible to justify controlling Michelle. He controlled what she ate, what she did, how she would talk, what she would wear and who her friends were. Michelle dressed like a doll with big poofy lace dresses and frilly socks even in high school. She got bullied a lot. She wasn't allowed to go to sleepovers or hangout at a friends' house. Her schedule was the same every day. Church, School, Home, repeat. Her parents smoked cigarettes a lot. She hated the smell so much she started hiding the cigarettes. Pauline had enough. Pauline whooped her with a wooden spoon until it snapped in half and sent her to her room without supper. Michelle resented them for how they controlled her. Every aspect of her life was decided for her. When she was eighteen all she wanted was to escape. She fell in love with her best friend Arthur. Arthur was an escape. For the first time in her life, she felt heard. Michelle moved in with him and by the time she was nineteen they got married. Michelle was pregnant. She was scared to be a mom. She didn't want to be smothering like her parents. She loved the idea of being a mom. They had a baby girl and named her Paradise. Michelle and Arthur were happy, but they fought a lot over money. Michelle wanted a lush lifestyle because she was used to Pauline and

Rice providing everything for her. She was used to having everything done FOR her. She loved to buy expensive clothes, jewelry, and makeup. Sadly, Things changed fast when Arthur started having health problems not long after paradise was 2 years old. He was losing his memory. what he did remember was different than how it happened. Michelle and Arthur started fighting a lot more. Michelle thought it would be funny to hide things that Arthur was having problems keeping up with like his car keys, shoes, watches. Gaslighting Arthur was her new favorite game. She could hide something and when he looks for it say, "look I found it! you're crazy" after pulling it out of the freezer she stuck it in. It made things worse. Arthur was paranoid and agitated. Fights went from verbal to physical. Michelle admittedly started most of the fights. She wouldn't let things be when Arthur tried to flee to calm down. She enjoyed verbally degrading him. Pushing him to that point. Telling him he was less of a man for having health problems. Arthur was diagnosed with schizophrenia. He was hallucinating. Michelle filed for divorce and full custody of Paradise. It was a bitter split. Arthur had filed for full custody of paradise. A nasty custody battle began. Wave after wave she couldn't get a break. Arthurs family testified against Michelle. Saying she was a helpless abusive alcoholic who pawned Paradise off on any and everybody. They weren't wrong. Michelle did the only thing she could have done, she used Arthur's diagnosis against him. She was granted Full custody. Arthur was allowed every other weekend visitation only. Arthur after the divorce, figured himself out in life and began dating a man. He was Gay. Months after their breakup, Michelle started dating an old high school boyfriend named Bologna. Bologna was her first "true love."

They had dated when they were sixteen. The ONLY reason they broke up was because Rice and Pauline didn't like him. Michelle loved him so much she got a rose tattoo with his name at 17. She paid greatly when Rice and Pauline found out. Tattoos were a big deal. In her parents' eyes it was blasphemous, the worst of the worst. Bologna got arrested. Him and his friend smoked crack and robbed a gas station at gun point. Bologna was fucked. They locked him up in the penitentiary. He was looking at 10 years. Michelle tried to make things work at first, but she could feel the cupcake phase fading fast without someone to provide for her and give her the constant attention she sought. She'd visit Bologna as much as possible, but life isn't easy when you're a single mom. One day as she was leaving visitation, she met a man. He was just getting out for attempted murder, aggravated battery, possession of controlled substances (meth), stalking, resisting arrest, trespassing and theft. His name was Pearl. He was charming. He knew how to talk. He presented himself good even though he was dangerous. I think that's why Michelle liked him. Michelle's parents controlled her childhood so much that in her early adulthood she had poor impulse control. Everyone warned her about Pearl, but Michelle wants what she wants. Their relationship was quickly intimate. Michelle's daughter paradise was left at daycare or pawned off on family so Michelle could go out with Pearl. Paradise was young but she saw the pattern. It was obvious Mom prioritized her new boyfriend. She was always a self-centered person. I'm sure Michelle didn't view it that way. She was one of those mothers who would claim motherhood was SO difficult she had to "Take a break." Taking a break is fine but every day? No. Michelle always had to find an excuse to get fucked up. She didn't have anything that made her feel good but attention, alcohol, and drugs. Of course,

Bias. I'm her second daughter narrating our entire lives. You'll see the pattern as the story

goes on.

Chapter 2
Fatherhood.

Pearl is a crackhead felon with violent tendencies. He's misogynistic, chauvinistic, and condescending. When he gets high, drunk, or going through withdrawal its worse than usual. He's an asshole all the time. His family dynamic wasn't exactly picture perfect. Pearl's mom Jane killed herself. She has no death certificate, and no one knows where she's buried. Her story is sad. Pearls dad Hux was a sniper for the navy during the Vietnam war. Jane and Hux met when he was on a break from deployment. They got married and quickly had four kids back-to-back one girl and three boys. Genie, Pearl, Ryan, and Kane. Hux was away a lot. It tore up the marriage. Jane and Hux got divorced. 7 months after the divorce, Jane turned all four of her kids into group homes that same day she took her own life. I've thought about her often wondering why? Was the stress of four kids too much? Was she financially struggling? Did she have postpartum depression? No one will ever be able to answer those questions. No one cared about Jane. No one spoke about her and bringing her up didn't ever go well. Hux didn't get his kids. In fact, he disappeared for 5 years working on an oil field in Africa. He knew the kids were in foster care being abused and neglected, he didn't care. Physical abuse, verbal abuse and sexual assault is common in group homes. Everyone pretends like the foster care system is a place that saves kids but most of the kids in the system suffer. The group homes split the siblings up. Pearl and Ryan were together, Genie and Kane were in a separate homes. Things were so horrible for Pearl and Ryan they ran away. Genie aged out of the system and worked hard to secure a place for herself. Hux's brother Tommy was able to gain custody of Kane who was the youngest. He searched for Pearl and Ryan, but they were already gone.

Pearl dropped out of school in the seventh grade. Ryan and Pearl lived under a bridge. They stole food from stores and garbage cans. They did whatever they had to do to survive. They got caught stealing and were arrested. While doing time Pearl and Ryan made money by betting on themselves in fights. They made a lot of commissaries off these fights. Pearl and Ryan got into it with corrections officers after one of these fights and the boys beat the officers up. This was a huge mistake. After they were released, they went back to living under the bridge. One night the boys were woken up by police lights. The corrections officers had spread word about what they did. Two police officers sought for retaliation. The officers cuffed the boys and beat the shit out of them. Punching them in the face and kicking them over and over and over. Once the boys were bloody, they pulled out their guns and fired right beside their ears. One of the officers told them "Count your blessings we didn't kill y'all right here. Toss you pieces of shit in the bayou for the gators." Pearl and Ryan split up after this. Pearl was living behind a gas station convenience store. He got caught stealing from it. They called the cops. Pearl had a problem with authority. He didn't like adults; he didn't trust them; he certainly didn't respect them. Louisiana in the eighty's was different. Physical punishment was quite common for disrespect towards an elder. Pearl fought the cops, which made his case more severe than it was. He couldn't stay out of trouble constantly partying, doing drugs, and getting into fights. After he got out again for petty theft he was living with a girlfriend for a while until he started beating on her. She filed a restraining order. Pearl violated the order and got 60 days. He ended up getting locked in the penitentiary for attempted murder after he closed a man's arm in his car and began to drive off with him in it. Now you're wondering why the fuck would he do that? There are three sides to every story. The two perpetrators and the truth. Pearl said this guy at a party was disrespecting him. They started fighting and he was winning. When he tried to leave the guy tried to sneak him, so he started to drive off with his shirt caught in the window. They called it attempted murder. Pearl always told this story and said It was a big misunderstanding. The truth? Pearl had a huge ego. He was fleeing after he started a fight and got his ass whooped. Somehow pearl rolled this guy's arm up in his car window cause the guy was chasing his sorry ass. Pearl held onto his arm and rolled it up in the window and drove off with him stuck at high speeds. Severely injuring and nearly killing him while drunk and high on meth. When he got arrested, he fought the police again. It only made things worse. Louisiana police beat the shit out of him. On pearls court date he told the judge to go fuck himself, so he went to the penitentiary at only 17 years old. He also managed to get his girlfriend April pregnant. He was not exactly father material. Pearl's girlfriend named the baby Chris. He was locked up when Chris was born. Pearl got into a lot of fights because of his attitude. He was 5,6 with long black hair, covered in scars from fights on his hands, arms and head. His shitty tattoos were hand poked with a paperclip and ink made from ashes mixed with toothpaste swirled together. Pearl was released after serving his 4 years. He met Michelle right as he was being released. He used his charm to convince Michelle to go on a date with him. Michelle would leave her daughter paradise with various family members so that they could get fucked up at a bar or a party. Michelle felt alive to be with Pearl. He was dangerous, it was exciting for her. It did not take long for Pearls true colors to start showing. He was deeply insecure, misogynistic, and violent. Pearl is a chauvinist, which is a person who believes that men are superior to women. Pearl viewed Michelle as a tool for him. A servant. A housekeeper. A possession. Pearl did not waste any time getting violent with Michelle. Michelle did not seem to have any real ambition to leave. It sounds fucked up, but she liked the fights. The attention she got afterwards. Pearl would always be nice. Michelle's family and friends would be concerned. She enjoyed the rush of the fight. Sometimes she would push his buttons just to see how far it would go. She was fearful too that one day it would go to far. He had hurt her severely before. She loved him.

"We're just going to the bar who are you trying to look good for?"

"I thought I looked nice" Michelle snapped. Pearl loudly gritted his teeth. This switch was immediate. The tension in the room was heavy enough to suffocate. Michelle tried to flee the room. Pearl grabbed her by her wrist and squeezed. He maintained eye contact, moved her hair gently from her face. He softly said.

"I like this better."

He handed Michelle one of his baggy tee shirts and a pair of her jeans. Pearl and Michelle left silently for the party. The Alcohol, weed, coke, meth, and rock music was unlimited. Michelle claims never tried anything before she met Pearl. That was a fucking lie. Michelle had tried plenty of things. She wanted to give off an innocent vibe being corrupted by this big bad felon.

She always kept the victim persona. The innocent. She hides her greed and mischief well.

Pearl did have a way of pressuring people to do things. He could not spell manipulation, but

he was a mastermind at it. They fought all the time. Pearl was always calling Michelle a slut,

whore, a bitch. In retaliation Michelle would pick out his insecurities, calling him short, broke,

a loser. She loved to press those buttons. She knew exactly what to say to trigger someone.

She could smell the insecurities on them. Something as small as those words were more than

enough for Pearl to feel entitled to lay hands on her. He would slap Michelle, punch her, push

her, choke her, throw things at her, throw her downs. He had broken multiple bones and

locked her in rooms several times. Michelle always made up an excuse for Pearl. He knew all

the right things to say to make her good and all the right things to say to make her feel like

absolutely fucking nothing. When Peal would butter her up, she felt like the prettiest happiest

luckiest loved woman on earth. When Pearl showed his real colors, he tore her apart. She felt

ugly, stupid and like no man would want her. He would often throw it in her face that she had

a daughter. No one would want to be with her to help her raise someone else's kid. Especially

a schizophrenic gay man's kid. Pearl did not hold back his misogynistic, racist, and homophobic

thoughts. He polluted Michelle's mind with hatred and Bias. After the fights Pearl would

pretend like nothing happened. He would buy wonderful things like jewelry or flowers, but

he'd never said sorry. Saying sorry meant owning up to wrongdoing. He did not do anything

wrong because Michelle was his property. You can do whatever you want with your property.

Pearl did not like Arthur 1. he was a man who had been with Michelle and two. He's homophobic. His dislike for Arthur bled over to Paradise. She, from such an early age, was put

in a situation where she was told to pick between parents. Honestly neither parent was truly

100% capable of being a good parent to her. Michelle and pearl were fighting one day when

Michelle was 7 months pregnant with Pearls child. Pearl punched her in the face, choked her

and kicked her over and over. Michelle gave birth to a still born. She kept this secret for a long

time. He was supposed to be my older brother. He never got the chance because of my piece

of shit father. The secrets we keep...sometimes they come out on their own anyway. Michelle

would have never in a million years told anyone publicly Pearl beat her so bad causing the

miscarriage but he did. That baby deserved his story to be told. He had a beating heart. He

could hear everything that happened to him. He deserved better than both of our shit

parents. Michelle covered up what Pearl had done. She didn't speak about it for years until it

was beneficial for sympathy from her kids. After the stillborn, within months Michelle got

pregnant again accidentally. Michelle gave birth to a baby girl named Faye. That's me. The

earlier years in my life are facts I have had to gather from my family members because my

parents are incapable of being honest. There are a lot of gaps. They would rather cling to their

lies than reflect on the horrible things they have done. Michelle and Pearl were not prepared

when they had me. They barely took care of Paradise. Honestly, the only reason Paradise had

clothes was because her dad Arthur would buy them for her. Michelle, Pearl, Paradise, and

Faye were all living at Pearls sisters Genie's house who also had three children of her own.

Genie was always watching us while mom and dad would leave to party. They pawned us off

whenever they could. We were an inconvenience that always needed something from them.

Genie was a saint despite the lies dad and mom tried to spread about her. After one long

night of drinking and doing meth the two jackasses came back to the house arguing loudly.

The arguing got worse and worse to the point where Genie confronted them. She was holding

3-month-old me. Genie told mom and dad they needed to keep it down or leave. Mom drunk

and high started talking crazy to Aunt Genie telling her "You don't talk to me like that I'll

whoop your ass bitch." Genie says, "fuck you bitch get your junky ass out of my house."

Michelle throws a glass plate that skidded the soft spot at the top of my head. She almost

killed her own 3-month-old daughter. If you do not know babies at that age have a huge soft

spot on the top of their head where the skull has not fully developed yet. One wrong move

and it will kill the baby. Genie set me down and started throwing hands. Genie within seconds

had my mom on the ground and was beating the fuck out of her. Pearl stepped in and

punched his own sister in the face as hard as he could repeatedly until she fell to the ground

and then he stomped her over and over. Michelle got up and helped stomp her. Paradise and

all of Genie's kids our cousins saw the entire event and begged them to stop. Genie was

rushed to the hospital for internal bleeding. She almost died. She told grandpa Hux and Uncle

Ryan what Pearl and Michelle had done. Uncle Ryan was pissed. How could Pearl do this to his

own sister especially considering they were living in her home? Ryan found Pearl and

whooped his ass. Pearl will deny this, but my cousins saw it. Genie obviously kicked them out

of her house. They were homeless. The shitty thing about them being thrown out was that

paradise and Faye were also homeless. No one called CPS. No one attempted to save Paradise and Faye. Everyone was okay with Pearl and Michelle leaving. Pearl and Michelle did not want to stay in the state long enough to find out If Genie was pressing charges. They fled the state and moved from Louisiana to Illinois. Michelle BEGGED her parents Rice and Pauline to let all of us live together. Michelle and Pearl moved into Rice and Pauline's basement. It lasted 2 years. Rice and Pauline hated Pearl. They knew he was beating Michelle and he was a dead beat. Rice was very clingy to Faye. Always talking about how beautiful and nicely she was developing along at only 3 years old. Grandma Pauline pulled Mom aside and told her we needed to go. Finally, mom and dad moved us into a small apartment. I remember when we were moving in, I was sitting on the bare wooden floor of the living room. It was completely empty except for a BIG old timey tv with a VCR. I remember watching Atlantis while mom and dad fought about moving things. Michelle found out she was pregnant again. She gave birth to a baby boy. They named him Dean. Dean was the biggest crybaby from birth. He was annoying. He cried nonstop. He barely slept. It took years to figure out that Dean was allergic to milk and his tummy was always upset. Pearl was not happy about Dean. He was sickly and a crybaby. He was everything that Pearl viewed as unmanly. Pearl's Chauvinism meant that he had expectations for what boys were supposed to be. Dean did not meet those expectations from birth. He already had given up hope on Dean. Pearl could not stand it when Dean would cry. He thought about smothering him and starting over. Trying for a new son. Michelle was scared pearl was going to kill Dean because of how aggressive and agitated he got during his crying fits. Pearl muffed Dean a few times. He would hold his big oaf hand over Deans nose and mouth while Dean was screaming to silence him blocking his air flow. I remember a few times counting the seconds scared he would never move his hand. I'm sure he did worse than I remember, but mom and dad will keep that secret. With the lack of sleep, they fought more than usual. Pearl regularly hit Michelle. He lost his job. He kept showing up late and smelling like alcohol. Operating heavy machines and welding equipment under the influence isn't smiled upon. Michelle begged Rice and Pauline to let us move back in again. I don't remember very much just brief moments of Grandpa Rice sexually abusing me. He started molesting me. Calling it games. He would reward me with sweets my parents didn't usually let me have. He told me I couldn't tell anyone about our games, or I'd be in big trouble. Michelle made a fake diploma for Pearl. She even created fake references downloading three different apps to generate fake phone numbers. He got a good paying welding job. He was making $40 an hour. He wasn't home much because he was working. He started drinking again so on the weekends the fights between him and mom echoed in the entire house. Grandma and Rice started fighting about how much they hated Pearl. They wanted him gone but Michelle was never going to leave Pearl. Grandma really hated Pearl. He was loud, he was rude, he was a brute. She hated Pearl so much that she didn't like any of her grandkids except Paradise because she wasn't Pearl's biological child. Mom got a job working at a call center. She would drop us off at daycare. Go to school then go to work then pick us up and do it all over again. Mom and dad moved us into a small rental house. It wasn't big or fancy, but it was our own place. Dad started becoming more aggressive towards Mom because he could tell she didn't need him anymore. Mom was making enough money and had a system that worked well enough that she could leave him. This made him feel insecure and angry. Every day when Mom would come home, she'd cook a meal for Dad and wait for him to come home no matter how tired she was. The first thing he did when he got him is grit his teeth without saying a word to Mom. Walk over to the fridge and get a chilled beer. He sits at the table and looks disgusted at the meal Mom's prepared regardless of what it was. She asks.

 "So? How was your day? What did you do at work today?"

Pearl through gritted teeth "why are you in such a giddy mood who got your panties wet?

" Michelle ignores him "Do you like the brisket? I slow roasted it during the day so it would be just how you like it."

Pearl laughed "Were you alone in a room with him? What's his name? who's got you smiling like that and acting like that? fucking somebody instead of working whore? Is that what you do? lie to my fucking face like I don't see what's going on here." Pearl shoved his plate off the table. The echo of the glass shattering on the ground woke up Dean. Dean was crying.

 "Are you serious Pearl? WHY?! There is no one else" she sobbed. Pearl stood up and grabbed Michelle by her hair and slammed her face on the counter. She fell over from the force.

"Go shut that fucking baby before I do. clean up this shit up woman."

Peal stepped over Michelle and hocked a logy on the floor. Michelle still dazed, picked herself up and quickly went to Dean's room. She hushed him back to sleep. I was four. I heard dad yelling and then the glass breaking and mom whimpering. I went to see what happened. Dad saw me. Shit.

"Come here girl. What do you know about mom's boyfriend? Is his name Jody? You know deans not your real brother your mom cheats on me all the time because she's a whore and a whore is a worthless woman. Well. Nothing to say?" Pearl slapped the back of my head "Go get me another beer stupid girl."

I nodded and went to the kitchen. I grabbed him two beers. Mom was cleaning the glass and food off the floor. She grabbed my arm hard and told me.

"Go back to bed right now GO!"

Mom snatched them from my hand and sternly said "Room now."

I walked back to my room. It was Friday. This was just the start. Weekends were the worst.

Chapter 3- Weekends.

Mom and Dad were tight on money. Grandpa Rice and Grandma Pauline knew this.

Grandpa offered Mom $50 a week for me to "help him out" with the paper route every weekend. I was 5 years old when this started. Every weekend my grandma would pick me up. we'd get a McDonalds happy meal then Grandma would make me take a bath. It's especially important in understanding my story that you realized Grandma knew what was going on. She aided in it. The lock in the bathroom was one you could unlock with your finger or a coin. The straight slot kind you know. Rice would come in while I was showering and watch me. He would masturbate. He would Molest me while I was in the shower. I hated it. It made me feel disgusting. I stopped taking showers. I found comfort in baths. I could use the cheap ass v05 shampoo Grandma got to make bubbles. I used this to try to cover myself. It didn't always work but it gave me a sense of comfort. I can't really explain it. I was five. Molestation and rape being disguised to a child as games. Unfortunately, it's common in addictive households because parents don't care about or pay attention to their kids. Rice would call me into his room and turn on animal planet. He turned the volume all the way up. No one needed to hear my screams. He locked the door. Afterwards Rice would bribe me. He would give me money or take me to get ice cream or buy me a toy. He would tell me he loved me. He would kiss me on the mouth and pat my head "Good girl." As fucked up as it was, he was the only one who told me he loved me or showed affection towards me. I would get rewarded for being a "good girl." Rice told me "This is our secret if you tell anyone about our games we can't play anymore. YOU will break up the family. Your dad will go back to jail and your mom will blame you" other times he told me "NO ONE WILL BELIEVE YOU." I was brainwashed. I didn't even understand what was happening. I was always scared, confused and alone. No one was going to believe me anyway. No one in my family gave a fuck about me. I knew that. Even at a young age without him telling me over and over. I was on my own. Mom didn't hug me, kiss me, or tell me she loved me and neither did dad. That really affects a young child's mind. Rice was a preacher. He was a "man of God." He used that to manipulate me. He used Christianity to protect himself. He would say that everything happens for a reason. It's part of God's plan. "God sees and hears all." "God only gives hardship to his strongest soldiers." He justified his actions by saying it was "God's will." I didn't get to have an opinion because voicing my opinion meant I was "talking back" to mom and dad which meant they would physically punish me for "disrespecting" them. Most of the time that meant getting slapped so hard you'd see spots for a few seconds but sometimes that meant the belt or the switch or standing in the corner for hours. It depended on their belief in the level of disrespect you had committed. Grandma and grandpa slept in separate bedrooms. I always wanted to sleep with Grandma even though she was mean. I clung to her for safety. She may hit me, but she didn't sexually assault me. In the middle of the night Rice would carry me out of her bed. She didn't always sleep through it. Sometimes she would tell Rice to leave me alone. It wasn't out of a place of kindness but out of jealousy. My grandma viewed me as competition. In her fucked-up eyes I was going to take her husband away from her. I have nightmares about it to this day. Rice in front of mom and grandma would smack my butt. He would say how nicely I was developing. Mom and grandma forced me to hug him and sit on his lap. If I didn't, I was" being mean" by denying his public affection. Shockingly the only person who ever said my grandfather's behavior was disturbing was my father. He said it was weird. Mom told Dad it was just his way of "Showing affection." stupid silly bitch. Dad lost his job again. We got evicted from the apartment. We moved back in with Grandma and Grandpa so now the abuse wasn't isolated to weekends. Although with more people meant more witnesses. I started getting bad rashes and regressing. Wetting the bed, a lot. Paradise and I shared rooms. She was not happy about my regression. Thankfully since Paradise and I shared a room together Rice's access to me was limited. He knew he couldn't get me out of my bed in the middle of the night when Paradise was with me because she could tell multiple people. Paradise had a court ordered custody agreement meaning regardless of whatever happened every weekend she would be at her Dad Arthur's house. I was an inconvenience and annoyance to her, but she was always a hero to me. She had no idea what was going on. Pauline was especially cruel to me. She hit me harder than anyone else. She gave me unusual punishments. She ridiculed me often. Grandma purposely excluded me from birthdays and holidays. She would buy my siblings valentine's day, Patrick's day, easter, fourth of July, Christmas, and birthday gifts but I never got anything. I would watch everyone celebrate wondering why I wasn't good enough to be included. Why everyone was so mean to me. Why everyone hated me so much. Questioning why I was even born. Grandma would talk badly about me to Rice in attempts to make him dislike me. She said I was a devil child. I was evil. There was something wrong with me. I wished it had worked but it caused her to become more bitter towards me when she realized she couldn't persuade him. She couldn't compete for his affection because he was a pedophile. Anyone who had fucking common sense would know that when a grown man who is twenty-eight starts dating a 13-year-old like he did with Pauline that he's a Pedophile. Rice's abuse was isolated to my bath time or the weekends. He had this big white van. He called it "big Bertha." If you don't know you pick the papers up for a paper route at about 3am. It's still pitch black dark outside and everyone's sleeping. After picking up the papers Rice would kiss Pauline goodbye who went to do her own paper route and we would leave in big Bertha. I'd be in the back of the van bagging the papers until the van pulled over. I knew what it meant. Rice found a perfectly isolated spot to play his games. I hated the weekends. I felt like I had no light or fight left. Everybody had taken something from me. I had nightmares constantly. Mom was fed up with my sleepless nights. She took me to the doctor after multiple rashes.

I told her "Grandpa makes me play bad games. I don't want to go on the paper route anymore. I don't want to help."

my mom said "We have a place to live now we have to be grateful. Faye, they're doing us a big favor Grandpa is letting us live with him and without him we don't have a place to live."

The pediatrician wanted to do more testing. Asking Mom if she thought I'd been sexually assaulted. Mom denied and acted appalled. She found a new pediatrician. She was more careful about describing things so that the doctor believed I was just a bad kid acting out because we had to move. Mom said I was wetting myself for attention. Perfectly leaving out the parts of drugs, physical and sexual abuse. Mom said that I was always acting out and doing things for attention. This was just one of those things. The doctor prescribed me rash cream but after the third time prescribing it wanted to schedule another appointment to run more tests. Mom never went back. None of the pediatrician's reported anything about me. I'd assume at this time because technically no tests were done. Now a days if I had gone through this it, I hope it would have been reported to child protective services. It was sloppy doctor's work. They should have reported it anyway. I started asking inappropriate questions. Mom grabbed me by the arm and ran me to the bathroom and shoved a full bar of soap in my mouth. She grabbed me by the face and told me "You don't ever say things like that ever to anyone!" She was furious. Mom said I was going to be the reason grandma kicked us out. She went to a third pediatrician. Managed to convince them that I was an "out on control" daughter. I remember sitting in the new doctor's office as she described me to the doctor. A hyper out of control child who never stopped talking, wetting herself and making up stories for attention. I wished I were dead. I wished I were never born. I wished she were dead. I wished she weren't my mother. I wished for so many things in that moment. I was placed on two mood altering ADHD medications at the maximum dosage at only 5 years old. Strattera and concerta. This only made things worse for me. I was groggy, irritated, nauseous and couldn't sleep. I stopped smiling. My brain felt like a blank slate. It was difficult to keep deep thoughts. I would start thinking and it would just fade away and my brain would blank out. It was like I was on auto pilot. I saw everything happening, but it wasn't me. I was living inside a body that didn't feel anything. I was a vacant shell. I didn't want to play with Paradise or Dean.

I thought things couldn't get worse. Surprise Mom was pregnant again. Another boy, Miles. Less than a year later she got pregnant again. When Mom was 7 months pregnant with Dad choked her on the table and broke all her ribs. My baby brother thankfully was fine. He was born on Halloween. I remember the day well. Grandma said Dean and I could go trick or treating. Paradise was with her dad. Grandma said she would take us as long as I could convince Dean to wear his woody from toy story costume. If I couldn't get him to wear the costume Grandma said, we wouldn't go. Dean was a huge crybaby. He was scared of the other people in costumes. It took me 20 minutes of convincing. I told him we're going to get a bunch of candy so put the costume on and let's get candy because we never get candy. Mom and dad aren't going to buy us candy. Dean agreed. He liked candy. He finally got dressed. Right as we're heading out the door with grandma her phone rings. Mom is in labor. Grandma said we aren't going trick or treating. We're going to the hospital. Within 2 hours our youngest brother Melvin was born. Miles was just a baby still. He was 10 months. Now there were two babies. Paradise, Dean, and I hardly got any attention unless it was negative. Mom spent most of her time fighting with dad, smoking weed and taking care of Miles and Melvan. She had bad postpartum depression after Melvin. She started binge eating. she developed type 2 diabetes. I was watching it all happen, but it didn't feel like I was present. It's hard to describe the feeling when there isn't anything. I was so heavily medicated. I felt like a robot on auto pilot. I didn't question mom and dad anymore. I didn't have the light I used to have. It all faded away. It was hard to process deep thoughts. It was like something blocked them. I stopped eating and lost a lot of weight. I stopped sleeping. I had constant migraines. The doctor wanted to remove me off the medications due to the side effects. Mom in front of me begged the doctor to keep me on the medication and try a lower dosage because this was "the most behaved I had been all my life and she liked me this way." This was the first time my mom ever even said she liked me. It almost made me feel something for a second. The pediatrician lowered my dosage and prescribed a sleeping pill. As I got older, I started refusing to take the medications. I would hide them under my tongue, cheek, spit them out or throw them up. Mom and dad would whoop me for it. She could always tell when I didn't take them because I had a personality and thoughts of my own. It was easiest with honey or a spoonful or yogurt. Everyday mom made sure she watched me take my medicine. My body started to reject the medication. I would Gag from the smell of the pills. I would gag trying to swallow them. Mom would make sure for 10 minutes I didn't throw them up. It was involuntary at this point, but she didn't care. If I couldn't swallow my own vomit back down, she'd make me take a second set of the medications. Mom got comfortable smacking me more often. I didn't have dramatic reactions. When she hit me, I was so numb I'd just stand there. She didn't like it If I would ask questions like "Why don't we have any money?" "Why don't we have a place of our own?" "Why don't you and dad have jobs?" WHOOP. She'd pop me right in the mouth. "It's none of your business." "it's not your place to ask that's grown business." The crazy thing is I was never scared of mom. She should have feared me. Although I was numb, I often had intrusive thoughts that almost always involved murdering her. I thought about suffocating her with her pillow the next time she got too high to stand. which happened at least once a week. I

thought about giving her too much insulin. I thought about stabbing her. I thought about

pushing her in front of traffic. I viewed mom as the problem. She was the root of all my

torment. At the center of every stem of abuse I received there my mom stood. Mom took out

her anger on me because she was pathetic and weak. I knew that. It sounds fucked up to think

of a person like that. I had no respect or love for my mother. I had watched my mom defend

my pedophile grandfather knowing he had sexually assaulted me. I had watched mom

purposely consume spoonsful of butter and sugar to trigger a diabetic attack for 5 minutes of

attention. I had seen my mom throw herself on the ground for painkillers. I had watched my

mom cry and beg my crack addicted father to come home after he had beaten us and her and

robbed us on Christmas. When I looked at my mom all I saw was a weak selfish person who

had kids out of desperation to keep a man.

Chapter 4: Death.

I'm not sure how well Michelle's biological mom Laurie knew her brother Rice because by the time I was old enough to ask questions. She had passed away from breast cancer. Mom bought us all nice clothes. She cleaned us up. Told us to be on our best behavior. It wasn't because she wanted us to look our best. It was because she cared deeply about trying to impress her arrogant siblings who treated her like dirt. Mom's siblings except for one of my aunts were bitches. They excluded her from everything. They didn't associate with her which just fueled Mom's extreme insecurities and thoughts of "I'm not good enough." We arrived at Grandma Laurie's funeral. Moms' siblings didn't even greet us. They stared. It was like we were an oddity that didn't belong. It was painfully obvious. They all felt like Mom shouldn't have been there because she was adopted out. We sat next to Grandma Pauline and Grandpa Rice. Rice didn't even shed a tear about his own sister. Mom nudged me to get up and tell my brothers to get up. We all walked with mom to the open casket. This was the first time I saw a dead body. Laurie was a stranger to me and yet here I was staring down at her corpse watching my mom cry over somebody she never knew. I knew Laurie discarded her like trash, so I didn't understand why she felt so sad and not angry. I felt sad seeing mom cry. In that moment I deeply felt bad for mom. I wished I could take her pain away, but I was just an inconvenience and annoyance to her. The best thing I could do was stay out of the way and do what I'm told. Mom went into a depression. She started sleeping all day, binge eating more and letting things go at home. Dad being the chauvinist he is which as I said before is a person who believes men are superior to women felt it didn't matter what my mom was going through it was her duty/purpose as a woman to clean up after his funky ass. Mom and Dad started fighting a lot more because dad would just keep calling her fat and lazy picking at her that a dead mom who didn't even raise you isn't a good enough reason to be sad. Mom had gained a lot of weight, so it was easy for dad to get under her skin. Mom started sticking up for herself she would call him a dumb lazy balding crybaby bitch. Dad would hit her or start destroying the house. If my siblings or me were in the way, he would hit us too. Mom started calling the police officers and having him arrested. I used to feel guilty that I was happy when the police would take him away. I knew things would be quiet at home for a while. Mom would always drop the charges. She'd let him back in the house like nothing ever happened. Eventually Mom started to shake the funk. She decided to go back to college to attempt to be a paramedic. She was doing well in school. Dad was making things difficult on purpose because anytime Mom did anything to better herself it made him scared that one day, she was going to leave him. He would destroy or hide her school supplies, schoolbooks, and assignments. He told her repeatedly she should drop out. She wasn't smart enough to pass. Eventually she caved in. She dropped out. She gave up. She only had 3 months left of schooling, yet she gave up. She fell back into another depression. At this point Michelle was the unhealthiest and heaviest she'd ever been. She was five foot 4 and 420 pounds. Her diabetes was out of control. She hadn't done it for a while but again started to not take her insulin to trigger an attack. Telling us she just wanted to die. Let her die. Nodding in and out of consciousness. I would have to run, get her insulin, measure it out, inject her or call 911. I'd get beat for it later. Mom didn't want me to do anything. I was just supposed to let her die in front of my three brothers and me. I hated my mom. She took my voice away, she made me take on all her responsibilities, she sold me to my grandpa every weekend and forced me on medications she knew made me feel awful. I thought about not helping her. Even though I did hate her I didn't really want her to die. What would happen? Would dad leave? If he did, would that mean grandma and grandpa get custody of us? Would we go to the horrible foster care homes dad talks about? Suicidal threats were a regular thing with both of my parents. My dad tried to kill himself multiple times. Usually whenever mom would talk about leaving him. He, just like my mom always made it into a huge spectacle. They wanted my siblings and I to start panicking and crying over the thought of them dying. They enjoyed the attention. I started to think about killing myself at age 8 years old. My parents and Grandparents always talked about how after you die if you're good you go to heaven. I knew I was a good girl. I always did what my parents and grandparents asked of me. I prayed to God every night. Wishing for him to save me and take me away. I prayed so hard with wishes for safety and a better life. I would fill with so much emotion I would cry. I remember thinking that not even God listened to me. I was so insignificant that not even God had time for me. I took ten of my mom's allergy pills and thought it was enough to kill myself. I said goodbye to our cat and dog and all my stuffed animals. Within an hour I got violently ill. I felt like a complete dumbass. I thought to myself God is laughing at how fucking stupid I am. I threw up on the ground in the hallway. Dad came out of his room. He slapped the back of my head so hard I fell knees first into my own vomit and yelled at me for not making it to the bathroom. Mom heard dad yelling and got up. She shockingly helped me clean the throw up. She even gave me a Gatorade from her secret snack stash and a bucket. She said to stay in my room and don't come out. I remember it was a Friday. I didn't have to go to my grandparents' house because I was "sick." It was worth mom only feeding me toast for 2 days. Mom brought in a pregnant stray kitty from outside. She's getting a bigger belly every day. Mom says we aren't keeping all the kittens, but I hope I get to keep one. Abra had six kittens. I loved them all, they were so adorable. My favorite kitten was this little black kitty I named shadow. I begged my mom to keep him he was the one. My mom said I could keep him. For 2 weeks I slept on the floor feeding him, petting him, and taking care of him. When I got home from school one day, I found out my parents gave away all but two of the kittens. She kept two grey twin kittens. She got rid of shadow. I cried and cried. I wanted him so badly. I had proven I could care for him. I started using my sadness to care for the other kittens because they were still extremely sweet and cute. I woke up and went to check on the kittens and one of them was stiff. He died. We never knew why but we had to bury him. I felt like my heart had been shattered. Death was cruel. Death was unpredictable. I was curious about death. Would I start over? Would I go to heaven? Would there be nothing? Would nothing be so bad? Was there a God waiting for me? If there was a God, why didn't he answer my prayers? I'd pray until the tears couldn't stop. I'd pray until I felt my heart sink into my stomach. I put all my soul into my prayers begging for help. I never felt heard. Someday I'd have a lot of questions for God.

Chapter 5
Addiction.

Mom and dad smoked a lot of weed together. They also smoked meth. Often, they would smash pain killers and mix them with weed in the joints. When they smoked those kinds of joints, they were so high they would be barely conscious. They would sleep during the day. If my siblings or me made any kind of noise to disturb their high sleep Dad would beat the shit out of us. Dad didn't try to hide it but whenever my siblings and I saw mom smoking she would say the joint was a cigarette. It didn't smell like my dad's Marlboro reds in a box, I was young enough to believe her. My mom was working at a plasma donation center. She would evaluate people and document their patient information to see if they were eligible to donate. You get paid to donate plasma. Sadly, a lot of people who abuse substances sell their plasma. VERY Ironically mom's job was to prevent addicts or anyone with an underlining condition from donating. She would work nine, sometimes 10 hours since dad didn't have a job. Dad lost his job because he was drunk. He would down a twenty-four pack of corona beers in an hour. He would be so wasted he couldn't walk or talk straight. He always claimed he never remembered what happened the night before. How ironic he never remembered what he did. While mom was at work dad had a friend named Burl over. Whenever he was over the smoke smelled so bad. It was because dad was smoking crack in the house. When mom got home dad was talking in riddles threatening to kill all of us. Mom could smell the crack in the room still and she immediately started searching around the house to find whatever he was doing. Dad was so cracked out that he went right over to his stash and checked to see it was still there. Mom grabbed his stash. She yelled at my brothers and I to go upstairs. We sat at the top of the stairs huddling together listening to our parents screaming at each other. Hearing loud bangs, things being thrown and then them hitting each other. She called the cops and had him arrested. While dad was on his way out with the cops he said, "bye kids I love you your mom doesn't love me or want me to be your dad anymore". While he was in jail it was so quiet in the house. Mom was working hard. The bills were behind due to drugs abuse. my mom was looking for smaller places for us to live. Mom dropped the charges. I don't know why but she was shocked when he didn't come home. Dad went to the trap houses to score. He was gone for months on a crack binge. Mom looked for him. Asking around if anyone had seen him. She couldn't believe he picked crack over her. Mom told us If dad comes home to call her immediately. Don't call the police. While she was at work dad came home. He was begging at the door. He peeped through the mailbox slot. "Faye let me in, its dad." I stepped back from the door. "Faye get back here and open this fucking door." I froze in fear. "Did your fucking bitch mom tell you to do this? Miles, Dean, Melvin?! LET ME IN. LET ME IN. THIS IS MY FUCKING HOUSE. LET ME IN." He started kicking the door. I ran and grabbed the phone. I called mom.

"Dad came home and he's kicking in the door."

The noise stopped.

"I don't know where he is I think he's trying to find another way in."

I was so scared. I knew when Dad got in, he was going to hurt me. Mom told me to tell the boys to hide upstairs. She was ten minutes away. She was leaving work now. She hung up.

She didn't care what happened to my brothers and I because if she did, she would have called 911. All my selfish bitch mom cared about was trying to talk my toxic ass Dad into staying with her sad desperate ass. My heart was pounding out of my chest. I started hearing the kicking sound again. This time it was coming from the back door. Our dog moose who was an exceptionally large dog was barking. He never liked my dad because he was abusive. Dad had kicked moose, thrown stuff at him, and punched him a few times because moose attacked him for hitting mom. *THUD* the door fell. I knew it from the sound. He kicked the door down. He was inside the house. I heard the muffled voice of someone else my dad said to them to "wait here." "You stupid fucking girl I told you to open the fucking door. I hurt my fucking foot because you won't let me in my own house, what you going to act like your stupid bitch mom?" Dad was approaching me fast, and he was about to smack me. Moose jumped up and attacked him. Moose was fighting my dad with all his might. He protected me. Dad was getting chewed up. His arm was bleeding. He grabbed a wooden closet rod that had been confiscated from my brother's room and he started hitting moose. Moose cried out in pain and my dad kept hitting him over and over and over and over and over and over. I was screaming at my dad telling him "No stop." Grabbing his arm trying to stop him with all I could. He just knocked me over. I heard Moose's bones crunch. He hit him one final time in the head and the noise it made is something that haunts me to this day. It kills me to think about this. Moose was unconscious on the ground. He wasn't making any noise. He was twitching. I was crying so hard I could barely breath. I was petting moose's bloody head just telling him I'm sorry and he was a good boy. I was ten. I tried so fucking hard, but I still feel I didn't do enough. After that day I wanted Dad to die. I thought of a million ways to kill him myself. I wished I had the nerve to do it. I was terrified of my dad. I knew mom would never end things because she was too weak. She would always keep him around. Mom got home 20 minutes after I had called her dad already had left with all the shit he stole from the house. TV's, DVD players, clothes, mom's savings. Mom saw me on the floor petting Moose. Just crying trying to console him. Mom saw the condition Moose was in. She got down on the ground with me and him and cried. She said she would never let dad back in the house after what he did. Moose survived but he had brain damage. He was never the same. He couldn't walk straight. He was afraid of everyone. He peed and pooped when he walked. He didn't know his name or any commands like sit or down anymore. He was barely alive. Mom being the dumb gullible whore she is forgave dad and slept with him the next day. She let him back in the house like nothing happened. Dad chained moose up outside that day. The next morning, he was gone. They claimed he ran away. The truth? Dad untied his leash and threw him in the street. I heard mom and dad talking as I stood eavesdropping from the top of the stairs. I don't know what happened to him after that. Dad told mom he wanted to get sober. He wanted them to be together because they were "meant to be." Mom fell for the bullshit. She let her guard down. Dad cleared the house of everything that was left. Stole all of moms' cards and every dollar in her bank account. Mom was completely broke. She had to beg Grandma for money to feed us. Grandma wasted no time convincing mom she needed to divorce dad because he was a useless druggie. She never liked him anyways. I was hoping

Mom would go through with it but after all the times she let him in I knew she wouldn't.

Grandma felt like she had an "in" with her daughter by helping her in her time of need. She

didn't do it out of kindness but out of hopes that she would be continuously needed. Grandma

paid for the divorce paperwork. Mom served Dad the next time he showed up. I remember

Dad started crying and begging to come back home. Mom tried to close the door. He stuck his

hand in the door trying to force his way inside. She closed the door on his hand. Hard. His

hand was bleeding.

He was crying saying "I'm hurt, I thought we said forever in sickness and in health."

just saying typical manipulative fuck boy shit.

"I'm bleeding woman can you at least let me inside, so I don't bleed everywhere."

My brothers and I were sitting on the top of the stairs snickering. Mom opened the front door

and thew a role of paper towels at his head and said,

"Get the fuck of my property or I'm calling the police."

Dad left. It was the most bravery mom had ever had. It didn't last. We went to bed early that

night per Mom's request. Later that night she let him come in while we were sleeping. They

came to an agreement. Dad went through withdrawal. He was more aggressive and volatile

than usual. It was so bad. The boys and I were hiding under our beds trying to stay out of his eyesight. No one wanted to be seen by him because he'd ask you to do things for him like he was a helpless infant. Get him water, make him a snack, change the tv channel for him.

Doesn't sound so bad right? He would berate you with insults the entire time and if you breathed the wrong way it was an excuse for him to hit you or throw things at you because you had an "attitude." It was far worse for Paradise, and I. He was looking for a reason to smack us already. His itch for hitting women wasn't scratched because Mom wasn't tolerating him beating on her anymore. We were free game. He was in what looked genuinely like agonizing pain. He looked crusty and gross. Puking, diarrhea, fever, hallucinations. After 2 weeks he ran out overnight. He went back with his friend Barl to smoke crack. Mom went chasing after him. She found him a couple of days later naked with some other crack whores. She chased him out smacking him and yelling at him while he was still naked. She cried for days. She kept saying that things were going to get better. For once I believed her. It was a long time before we saw dad again. Months. Mom was working hard, and I didn't have to go to my grandparents because Paradise and I had to watch Dean, Miles, and Melvan, they were too young to be left home alone. A week before Christmas dad broke into the house overnight. Mom told me to hide with the boys upstairs. she went downstairs. We hear mom screaming "no stop." loud bangs. Thuds. Glass breaking. After a few minutes Everything got quiet. The only sound left was mom crying. Dad stole all the money she saved for Christmas for us. Paradise, my brothers, and I hugged my mom as she cried. We said we don't care about Christmas we just care if he's gone. 2 weeks after this my dad shows up and claims he's realized family is what matters. My mom let him back in the house. He was trying to get sober. He went through withdrawal again. PUKING, DIARRHEA, FEVER, HALLUCINATIONS, IRRATIONAL ANGER. Dad stayed off crack but to kick the habit he started popping painkillers. He really liked the way Norco's made him feel. He started mixing the painkillers with heavy alcohol use. Dad stopped hitting my mom all together. He realized that by hitting her he risked going to jail again. She had him arrested over four times at this point. Dad began to focus his abuse on us his children. He didn't like women. He didn't respect them. He was still angry towards mom and his own mother. He took it out on Paradise and Me. Dad had a lot of rules for what he expected from paradise and I. Paradise, and I were supposed to clean, cook, do laundry, watch our three bad ass little brothers, and service dad whenever he asked for something. We also were expected to walk, talk, and sit a certain way that was "lady like." We weren't allowed to play video games because dad says that's for boys. Dad does an outfit check on paradise and I and tell us our "Ass looks fat in those change" "the boys will all be staring change" "you're trying to bring attention to yourself change." It was confusing because everything I owned in my closet was picked out by mom, dad, or grandma. I never picked out my own clothes. All my clothes were old and hand me downs. Thrifted from goodwill or given out for free at the food pantry. I wasn't allowed to have a say in anything. Not how I talked, walked, dressed, or felt. Dad would get incredibly angry if he thought paradise or I had an attitude. His idea of having an attitude was breathing too loudly or moving your head too quickly. He would swear you rolled your eyes or sighed. He would choke us against the wall, hold us by our face, slap us or shove us if he thought we so much as rolled our eyes or sighed.

He claimed we rolled our eyes truthfully; he just wanted an excuse to hit us. He enjoyed

punishing us. It became obvious when my siblings and I would all get a whooping exactly how

much dad enjoyed it. We have to go outside and pick a switch. A switch is a fresh flexible

branch from a tree that hits like a whip. It leaves cuts and bruises and scars on your skin when

used hard enough. When we were all getting whooped Dad would hit my brothers with the

switch over their pants five or six times even if they jumped or put their hands in the way.

When Dad whooped Paradise and me, he pulled our pants down. Bare ass. If we jumped or

put our hands in the way our punishment started over. Dad would laugh when we jumped or

would beg for him to stop, but he never did that to our brothers. Dad said it was gay to

whoop the boys with their pants pulled down. Probably cause he's a fucking pervert. The more

drunk he was the more likely he was to find a reason to spank my sister and me. His drinking

consumed him from the moment he woke up to the midafternoon when he passed out, he

was wasted. He would fall asleep on the floor and piss himself because he was so drunk. He

would get angry trashing the house saying mom was cheating on him. He'd destroy the whole

house. Eventually he broke every single door in the house. He punched holes in the walls.

Paradise stayed in her room often. She was scared to come out. Dean, Miles, and Melvin

stayed in their rooms when dad was like this too. Dad would call for me mostly to come

service him like a personal butler. He would want me to massage his back, tickle his crusty old

man feet, get him a drink then wait for him to finish it and get him another. He would make

Paradise and I walk to the local gas station or grocery store to get him a fucking pickle or honey bun. We only existed to serve him. He treated us like personal butlers not children. He would call us from our rooms to come downstairs to pick up something he dropped on the ground less than a foot away from him. Just for us to pick it up. It was annoying and degrading. It got to the point where we were all so scared of him, we would hide. It started with hiding under our beds but when we wouldn't come to him calling our names, he would drag us from under the beds. We had to get more creative with our hiding spots. We hid in cabinets. On the roof. Even in a ventilation duct. We pulled off an air duct vent in our brother's room and discovered an entire room filled with pink installation (fiber glass). It became a daily routine to hide in the vent away from our dad. He couldn't reach us inside because you had to be exceedingly small to get in the vent. It was our safe place. We brought toys in there and we would play in there all day while mom was gone. We tried our best to avoid dad. Dad's drinking really brought out his true colors. He told paradise and me that we needed to be taught a women's place. That's why he was so cruel to us. We had to learn that women had no value other than being a silent servant to a man. He constantly insulted us. My dad called me "stupid girl" more than he ever called me by my name. I was nothing more than a random female to him. Mom didn't care because the abuse had shifted from her to paradise and me. Why would she care about that? Afterall we were just government assistant checks to her at this point. She used the food stamp benefits she got from us by selling them to people for money. She'd give someone the food stamp card to use, and they'd give her cash. She used the money to fuel her and Dad's pill addiction. Once dad was back in the house and sober for

2 months, Mom's job didn't last long. Dad started accusing her of cheating. Every single day when mom got home from work, he would make comments about her cheating and start a fight. After the fights with mom, dad would find a reason to hit us. Mom sometimes felt bad sometimes. She knew he was cruel. She would offer to whoop us for him. Part of it was because she felt bad, the other part was because mom was a pick me. She wanted him to feel like she was capable of being just as cruel as he was. She would take us to her bedroom. She got out the belt out and would tell us to "cry like you mean it" because if it weren't believable dad would whoop you. She would hit the bed hard with the end of the buckle, so it made a loud cracking sound a few times. We would fake cry to appease dad's idea of "discipline." Afterwards mom would tell us to go into our room and stay out of sight. My memory has patches. It's part of what your brain does to protect you from dreadful things. Unfortunately for me my brain didn't block out enough. (This is a flash back). My memories really start at 5 years old which I think is typical. Elementary school wasn't that bad, but I only had two friends and one was Cuban and the other was African American and you're wondering why the fuck am I mentioning this? Why does that matter? It's no surprise that my White trash father on top of being a junkie and a misogynist was also a racist. When my dad found out who my friends were he pinned me against the wall. Holding me by my chin elevated off the ground. Staring me dead in my eyes "you aren't allowed to be friends with N*****s and B****Rs do you hear me little girl?" I knew my parents' beliefs were wrong. I didn't believe what they said. Sadly, this was my reality. This was something both my parents forced on my siblings and me.

We were indoctrinated to believe every stereotype you could imagine and every hateful ideology. They often justified their hatred with the bible but would never mention specific quotes. They would just say it was unnatural. They referred to people of any other skin color as beasts or wild animals. They constantly said that white people have no business being with anyone but white people. Perpetuating these harmful stereotypes that any person of color would harm me or pollute me. Diminish my value. Dad said he would disown me. Throw me out on the street from as young as I can remember his racism has always been prominent. I pretended to not be friends with Dari and Denisha but secretly I kept the friendship. I wasn't good at social interaction; they were so kind and amazing to me during our friendship. I was one time allowed to go to a sleepover although I had to lie to do it. My dad later found out later. I was beaten with a switch severely for being friends with a "Mexican." Dari was Cuban and her family was the kindest I had ever encountered. I often wished I had a family like my friends did. Their families didn't ridicule them. Their families didn't hit them. They didn't prioritize drugs. They had houses to live in. They had toys. They had clothes. They always had food. They had beds. My bed was on the floor without sheets, and it smelled like cat piss. I didn't even have a door to my room because my brother broke it down after dad broke theirs. They said if they didn't have a door, I didn't deserve one either. Every stereotype my parents told my siblings, and I about described my own parents. I had only ever been allowed to go to one other sleepover, which didn't happen until I was thirteen. Mom and Dad didn't want me talking about my home life. Dad told me what to say if anyone asked about what was happening at home. I was to immediately have my parents call and if I didn't, he would hurt

me. He would say that if we talked to counselors, teachers, or child protective services my

brothers and I would all be split up and go to separate homes and we'd never see each other

again. That the foster homes would be worse than home. That all your siblings would hate you

for breaking the family apart. He said I had things easy. I just didn't know it or appreciate it.

Dad constantly hit me, pushed me, and threw things at me over the smallest things. I knew

regardless of what I did he would find a reason to yell at me about how stupid and useless I

was. As I said earlier my memory in this stage from 5 to 10 is patches. Dad was sexually

abusing my sister. I don't know when it started. I'm done protecting abusers. I'm done being a

bystander. I'm done being a victim. My disgusting pedophile dad was sexually attracted to my

sister. Do you know how kindergarteners bully their crushes? That's why Dad constantly picked

at her. He sexualized everything she did. He called her ugly all the time to try and lower her

self-confidence because she rejected his advances. My sister was only eleven the first time I

remember my dad doing anything inappropriate to her. I don't want to dwell on it much as it's

her story to tell but I love my older sister very much. She didn't get a chance to speak up

about what was happening because Mom was quick to silence her. Mom was quick to cover

up the abuse. Mom was quick to gaslight everyone into thinking it's not a big deal for an adult

man to expose his little weenie to his stepdaughter and tell her to touch him. Paradise and I

didn't get along when we were younger because we didn't understand each other. When I

needed her, she saved me. I wished I could have done the same for her. My sister is one of the strongest women I've ever met. Dad said and did things a grown man should never say or do to a child. My father is a pedophile. There is no tip toeing around sexual assault to a child. My mom was a bystander who not only knew but let it happen. There was also a day my dad was extremely wasted. He called Paradise and I to come sit on his lap. I had to be nine paradise was thirteen. If we didn't comply to do what dad said he was likely to hit us, so we sat on his lap. He started feeling us up between our legs and grabbing our breasts saying how we were grown women now. I started crying because I knew what this feeling was. I knew where this was going. My grandfather had already been sexually abusing me for years. That hadn't stopped his contact had just been limited. I couldn't do anything but cry because I couldn't believe dad was just like Rice. He was a lot of things but a pedophile too. Damn. It hit hard. Even though I had seen him be creepy towards Paradise it never clicked until that moment. Paradise looked in my eyes. She saw the fear. Her big sister instincts kicked in. She grabbed my hand, and we ran out of the house. Dad was chasing us yelling at us to get back here or he was going to beat our ass. After a few minutes we hear dad and our brothers outside. "Find them now." There was a wooded area behind our house. We ran as fast as we could deep into the woods. I remember tripping hard and cutting up my knee. Paradise helped me up. We kept running. We hid inside a hallow tree and sat quietly. Dean, miles, and Melvin had no idea why they were searching for us. They were just doing what dad told them to avoid an ass whooping. They were screaming at the top of their lungs for us to come out. They had sticks waiving them in the air. To them it was a game. They had no idea what was happening. Dad kept saying for us to come out and "everything would be okay." It was clear the more time was going by the more he was panicking. He kept switching from "it will be okay" to "I'm going to beat your ass when I find you." He didn't want anyone to know he just molested his daughters. He was on his third felony meaning one more he goes away for life. That's all he cared about. After an hour of sitting, they finally gave up. We could hear dad yelling at the boys for "Being too useless" to find us. I felt bad. I knew they were going to get punished. Paradise had a track phone. She used it to call grandma. Grandma hated dad and me, but she loved paradise. Paradise wasn't around grandpa until she was about ten. A 10-year-old isn't as easy to groom as a 5-year-old. My grandfather picked me because it was easy. He was able to train me to be quiet and I had a mom and dad who didn't care about me. When I realized paradise was having grandma get us, I panicked. I didn't want to go there either. I hadn't really thought things through about what would happen if we ran away from home. I asked paradise if I could sleep with her because I was scared but the real reason was because I knew Rice wouldn't take me out of the room with Paradise in it. We were only at grandmas for a few hours before the police showed up. Mom called them and said we ran away. We weren't even asked by the police why we left. Paradise tried to explain but the cop interrupted her and said, "these are your parents, and you do what they say." When we got home dad gritted his teeth at us "you're lucky I'm not going to beat your asses I'm going to let your mama do it." Mom took us to her bedroom "what the fuck happened." I started crying because I knew she wasn't going to believe us no matter what we said. She already made up her mind we were bad kids. We were always going to be the problem. She was always going to pick him. Paradise explained dad molested us. Mom said at first "we must have interpreted it wrong" then when I explained as an 8-year-old that dad was touching me inappropriately she said, "we must have done something to give him the wrong idea". Yeah, his 13-year-old stepdaughter and an 8-year-old daughter did something to invite their 40-year-old dad to molest them. Fuck you bitch. It wasn't even 2 weeks later when I came home from school dad was yelling about bay leaves being gone. He was making red beans and rice. He knew paradise hated it. He said she must have hidden the bay leaves. When she got home from school, he started screaming at her about how she was an evil bitch who hid the bay leaves so no one else could eat the red beans and rice. Paradise snapped. "I didn't hide the bay leaves I don't know what YOU'RE TALKING ABOUT." Dad started choking her against the wall. Her face turned all red. I watched terrified. He threw her to the ground by her neck. "Get your fucking shit and get the fuck out of my house." Paradise left. When mom got home dad said paradise had run away. She called and reported her as a runaway. I hadn't seen my sister for a long time. I didn't know what happened to her. I was sad. I felt like she abandoned me. After she was gone dad was so much angrier towards me. I was now the target. I was the only girl in the house. Mom wouldn't tolerate hands being put on her, but she didn't give a fuck when it was her kids suffering. Dad was volatile. He tore my confidence apart. Told me how stupid and useless I was every day. I was forced to do chores constantly because dad said that was a woman's job. There was so much stuff paradise was forced to do that I didn't even realize it until she was gone. She left for her safety and happiness. Once Mom quit her job after Dad

kept accusing her of cheating things in the house declined rapidly. We were living in filth and

squalor. There were hundreds of mice, flies, and maggots. The sink was full of dirty dishes

because mom and dad didn't pay the water bill. There was no way to wash them. There was a

room in the back of the house we called "the laundry room" it was full of dirty clothes, bugs,

and mice. The conditions of the house were something you'd see on the tv show hoarders.

The laundry room had so many dirty clothes in it that the mice would eat the clothes. Dad

ordered me to clean the room. I started throwing everything away because it was ruined. In

the remnants of dirty laundry, I found dead mice that had crawled in the clothes and just died.

I found a dead kitten. It had been in there for a while. Decomposing. I cried as I cleaned it. I

wanted to bury it, but dad yelled at me and told me to throw the kitten in the trash. There

was roaches, maggots, and spiders. Dad came and slapped me because I wasn't cleaning

quickly enough. He slapped me again because I had an "attitude" for being slapped. A mouse

nest and I asked him what I was supposed to do? There were at least fifty baby mice. Dad

laughed "come on stupid girl." He took me to the basement and grabbed a mallet. He told me

to hold it. I was very confused. He stood over me. "Smash them." I looked down at the baby

mice who were cute and said "no." He slapped me on the back of the head. "' STUPID

FUCKING GIRL." I started crying hysterically. Dad called my brother Dean from upstairs. Dean

came over confused looking at the baby mice. Dad snatched the mallet from my hands. "DEAN

you need to toughen you up you're a fucking sissy I need you and your dumb ass sister to smoosh these baby mice and bag them up" Dean was only seven. He started crying because

he didn't want to kill baby mice either. especially in such a cruel way. Dad started screaming at

Dean "DO IT YOU FUCKING PUSSY." He said neither of us were going anywhere until we

smooshed them. I took the mallet, and I was trembling. I could barely hold it my entire body

was shaking. I was crying so hard my snot bubbles had snot bubbles. I swung the mallet with

my eye's closed but the sound of baby mice screaming, and the squish was so disturbing. I'm

still haunted by this incident. I threw up right there on the floor. Dad slapped my back so hard

I fell forward nearly landing in my own puddle of vomit. He was laughing "you did good girl

clean this shit up" referring to the pool of vomit in which I was kneeling. He snatched the

mallet from under me and gave it to Dean. Dean was bawling and begged "please dad don't

make me do this." I told Dad "It's okay I'll do it". Trying to spare Dean. He ignored me. He kept

yelling over and over until dean swung the mallet and squish a singular baby mouse. He made

us keep switching. Killing at least fifty baby mice. While he stood over us making sure we

killed them. Then he made us pick up their bodies and guts while he laughed at our discomfort

and disgust. Dad enjoyed making his kids mentally and physically suffer. I told mom what dad

made us do. It caused a huge fight. Dad waited until mom went to the food pantry the next

day and whooped us with the switch for snitching. With mom not working and dad drinking

every dollar we had things got worse. The water was already shut off, then the gas, then the

power. We still had to go to school even though we hadn't had a bath in a few weeks, we had

dirty clothes that smelled like cigarettes, mildew, and cat piss. Mom wouldn't brush my hair so

I had a huge ball of matted hair on the back of my head that went unchecked for months until I would see paradise. We all got bullied for bad hygiene at school. Teachers noticed. We had several calls home from school. My parents would gaslight the schools and say, "being poor isn't a crime we are just going through hard times." Our parents had a mortgage payment. Instead of paying it they decided to use the last bit of money they had from the multiple loans they'd taken out and food stamp benefits on Alcohol, Norco's and Weed. My mom liked being so high she could sleep all day and you'd think that would be a good thing with all the abuse, right? Wrong it meant we ate less and less because mom wouldn't get up to go to the store or food pantry. It meant we had to be quiet because if we woke her or dad up, we would be physically hurt. We tried to avoid dad. One extremely muggy day I accidentally woke dad up. He heard me opening a ravioli can to feed my brother with the handheld can opener. We heard his footsteps and hid in the cabinets. We waited until we heard him walk past us and ran upstairs to hide in the ventilation duct. He was so angry. We wouldn't come out. He tried to manipulate us by offering to get us McDonalds or sweets or saying he wouldn't be mad if we came out. We knew that was bullshit, so we didn't come out. Dad moved the boys bunk beds in front of the vent blocking us from leaving. We were stuck in the vent suffocating slowly for hours. I became claustrophobic because for hours we tried to move the beds from in front of the vent so we could leave. The room we were trapped in was too small for us to stand in. I went to a middle school on the west side. I was the opposite of hard. My parents had beat the confidence out of me. I didn't have any friends. I got heavily bullied. I was bullied so badly I was fearful of going to school. I got picked on for my clothes, my hair and being scared because I wouldn't talk. I was small, barely 4,9 and 100 pounds. I was an extremely

easy target. The girls at that school bullied me relentlessly. It made me hate going to school.

My grades dropped. School used to be my escape but now I was so scared I didn't want to go.

My brothers got a bus to school but I was .1 under the mile limit so I had to walk to school

every day. Our house was on the worst side of town. It was across the "projects" which are

exceedingly small apartments you get with government assistance for low-income families.

There was and is a lot of gang violence and drugs that still go on to this day in this area. I had

to walk to school by myself every single day. Beating sun, Rain, sleet or snow it didn't matter.

My parents wouldn't drive me and didn't give a single fuck if I went missing. Everyone knew I

walked to and from school. One day when I was on my way home three girls came up behind

me and hit me on the head with railroad rocks and proceeded to beat me until the back of my

head was bleeding. They didn't even know my name. Only one of the three girls had a class

with me, and it was a gym which had like over fifty people in it. The girl who had a class with

me said she didn't like me because I was a "Weird white bitch who didn't talk." She had her

two cousins help her jump me with railroad rocks. I kept begging them to stop as they hit the

back of my head over and over. I kept trying to walk away. I didn't try defending myself out of

fear of what might happen. A man driving on the road with his young kids in the car saw me

being beaten by these three girls. He stopped on the side of the road and chased them off. He

helped me up and drove me home. Dad came outside pissed because a strange man had given

me a ride home. The man explained to my dad that I had just gotten jumped and was on the ground being beaten with railroad rocks. Dad's attitude changed. He acted nice and shook the man's hand. He thanked him. Mom started crying. Making the situation about her of course. She asked the man for his phone number so she could file a police report. I begged my mom not to call the police because it was only going to make the bullying worse. Mom rushed me to the hospital where they said I had a concussion. The police arrived. Mom told them what happened. She gave them the man who witnessed its number and the girls all three got suspended from school. Not expelled. Suspended for 5 days. A single week. No punishment from the police unless I wanted to testify in court. I wasn't doing that. I ain't a snitch. When I got home from the hospital dad called me in the living room and told me to sit down. He gave me a 30-minute speech on how if I didn't go to school and fight those girls, he was going to whoop my ass. He wasn't joking. I was more scared of my dad's whooping's than the girls. The next week when they showed up at school. Everything happened so fast I couldn't even think straight I was completely consumed by my rage. The second I saw the girl who I shared class with I ran up on her. She was slacking. She had no idea I was going to snap that day. I am popping her face. Her cousin one of the girls who had jumped me snaked me. We got to fighting while the other girl was still leaned up against the locker. She was a lot bigger than me, but she was slow. We both had a fist full of each other's hair swinging. I ended up ripping out a huge piece of her sew in. She stopped swinging and started yelling because her real hair came out with it. She said she was done. I popped her one more time in her face and as I'm walking off, I see the third girl who jumped me. She was in the crowd but as the fight was dying down, she was backing through the crowd. This all sounds like a long ordeal but it happened so quick. I started following the girl through the crowd. I wanted my lick back. That adrenaline rush is crazy. Especially when people bullied you and hurt you physically your whole life. I ran after her. She bolted down the stairs. I chased her. Everyone in the school was watching. They weren't expecting the quiet girl to snap. I didn't even think I was capable of fighting. I thought for sure I was going to get my ass whooped. Just as I was about to kick the girl down the stairs a security guard came up and grabbed me. I broke free from his grip because I was flailing out of control and swinging. I grabbed onto the girl's hair. I was pepper sprayed by two other security guards. Obviously, I'm not superman when I got pepper sprayed, I let go. I started screaming that shit burned. They dragged me off. I ended up getting a 2-week suspension. A higher punishment than the girls got for jumping me. Whatever. I didn't give a fuck. For the first time in my life, I didn't take someone's shit. Dad was proud of me for once. When he picked me up from school, he congratulated me. When I came back to school no one bullied me. Everyone was nice to me and tried to be my friend. I found it disgusting, but I enjoyed having my peace. No longer having to hide in the bathroom for lunch. No longer having to worry about girls snickering about me when I walked past them. I had earned respect. No one fucked with me after that. The girls who jumped me got clowned constantly. Now they were getting bullied. Since the mortgage didn't get paid the bank reclaimed the house. Mom and dad told us 2 days before we were being kicked out that we were in fact being kicked out. My parents being the ignorant racists they are said it was

Obama's fault for giving all the jobs to immigrants even though they hadn't even applied to a single job. Mom said we were moving in with grandma and grandpa for a while. I was terrified. My grandfather would have unlimited access to abuse me. AGAIN. I felt my heart drop into my stomach. Grandma hated every one of her grandkids except paradise. Paradise was living at grandmas until she found out we were moving in. Paradise at 16 moved in with her boyfriend's family. Grandma made us all stay in one room in the basement even though she had two spare bedrooms upstairs. She wrapped the sofas in plastic wrap then put sheets over top of it because she said we were dirty. We weren't allowed upstairs. We were only allowed to be in the basement or outside. My grandfather didn't abuse me any extra other than on the weekends. I was incredibly stressed out. I knew what he was doing was wrong. I knew that no matter what if I told another adult outside of the family my parents were going to punish me or accuse me of lying. Mom suggested grandpa take me to and from school since I was now so far away, and I only had a month left. For the last month of school my pedophile grandfather took me to and from school. When he showed up to pick me up, he made sure to play country music loudly and yell for me. It was embarrassing and humiliating. I was so happy when the school year finally ended. It was starting to mentally tear me apart. I felt disgusted. I felt tarnished and broken. My dad always said a lady's worth was based on her body. Mine was constantly desecrated. My dad said rape was a girl's fault. She had to of done something to give the man the wrong idea. This dwelled in my mind. What did I do as a kid in diapers to entice a grown man? What did I do wrong? Why is God punishing me? I prayed so hard every night that things would get better. God never answered me. Dad was right. I was tarnished. I wasn't worth anything. I must have done something as a 5-year-old to deserve to be raped. It had to be me. I was always the center of the abuse so it must be me. How stupid does that sound? As an adult now I think about how 11-year-old me thought and it makes me so sad. If anyone else out there is feeling this way, please know you didn't do anything regardless of your age, your clothes, or demeanor. Its never an invitation to be taken advantage of. girl, boy, they/them you never did anything. You didn't deserve it. I hope you heal from it as I have started to. I hope someday you tell your story. It does get better. #METOO.

(MINI STORYTIME)

My dad is a chauvinist. A chauvinist is a person who believes men are superior to women. It's not like a misogynist. A misogynist is someone who just doesn't like women. A chauvinist thinks your entire existence as a woman is being a servant to men. You only exist to serve men. Cook, clean, have children. They view you as a possession to be controlled and owned.

My dad had no respect for woman. Not my mom and especially not my older sister and me. My brothers were taught by my dad they could do and be whatever they wanted if it was within his standards of manly. Unfortunately, that meant Paradise and I paid the price. The boys didn't know anything better other than what dad taught them. Mom and dad would leave for extended periods of time. Sometimes they would be gone for a few hours, sometimes a day, sometimes a few days. Whenever they were gone it was Paradise and I's job to watch the boys. Dean, Miles, and Melvan were bad as hell. Dad had taught them they didn't have to listen to women. They didn't have to respect them either. When mom and dad were gone the boys were demons. They would draw on the walls. Break holes in the walls. Run around naked. Break anything and everything. Get into mom and dad's snack stash. Destroy mom and dad's room. Anything the boys did no matter what. It was always Paradise and I's fault was always. Meaning the second they got home we were getting our asses whooped for whatever they did. It was EXCEEDINGLY rare they ever received actual punishment for the things they destroyed. When they did get punished for things like destroying my parents' room, we ALL got punished. Dad would line us up in age order. PARADISE, FAYE, DEAN, MILES, MELVAN. We'd get the belt. Dad would bring his arm all the way back. You'd hear the crack of the wind then feel the sting of the belt. Paradise and I got the worst of it. Ten licks minimum. The worst part was Paradise being before me. I could always tell how angry dad was based on how hard he whooped her. The worst part is knowing what's coming next and you must wait for it. After getting our asses whooped, we'd all be sent to our rooms which were across from each other. Not being allowed to make a sound. If we did dad was already mad, he'd have no problem whooping us again. My brothers and I's room had no door, so we'd sit in our rooms giving each other the middle finger. Writing notes that said fuck you to each other. Dean, Miles, and Melvan loved WWE. They used to play wrestling all the time. I could only play when dad wasn't home because he'd whoop me for playing a "Boys game." We'd wrestle on mom and dads' bed when they were gone. It went very wrong a few times. One time Miles and I were tag teaming Dean and Melvan. Mile's donkey kicked Dean and his head got stuck in the wall. We had to break the wall bigger to get his big head old. Another time Miles and Melvan were wrestling, and Miles picked up Melvan to Batista bomb him and it broke the entire frame of mom and dad's bed. We got the ass whooping of a lifetime. We were extremely poor due to mom and dad's substance abuse. Mom would cut all our hair. We didn't get to pick the style. Mom would get a strainer and place it on our heads and cut all the way across. We all looked like coconut heads. Bowl cuts for everybody. I had bangs so I looked like Dora the explorer. It was very unflattering. It didn't help with bullies at school. It was bad enough we smelled like weed, cigarettes and cat piss but we also had ugly ass haircuts. Melvan hated the way mom cut his hair. A few times he got ahold of scissors and cut his hair himself. When dad said it, he got out his clippers. He shaved Melvan completely shiny bald. The boys did whatever they wanted. It was difficult. I had all these rules, and they didn't. They would talk crazy to Paradise and me but when mom and dad left, we were addressing it. Fuck you thought this was? We were going to get whooped anyways mind as well make it worth it. My brothers and I and paradise fought all the time. We first fought BAD. The boys didn't understand from our perspective. They saw dad beat us all the time but because it wasn't them, they thought it was funny. Paradise and I regularly went without eating the boys would share a can of ravioli. We would walk to the gas station and steal honey buns or dollar donuts to feed them. We took beatings and made-up excuses on the days when dad was really drunk to save them. We tried our best despite them not understanding or even trying to understand what it was like to be in our shoes. We never got a thank you. We didn't expect one. We loved our little brothers. They weren't perfect. Neither were we. We tried our hardest to keep them safe and alive in a horrid situation. We did what we could.

CHAPTER 6
MOLD.

Living back in Grandmas basement Dean, miles, Melvin, and I had no beds. The four of us

shared a blow-up air mattress. Mom's raggedy flee infested cats Gizmo and Tippy kept

popping it so it had a bunch of duct tape over the holes. Overnight the bed would go flat so in

the morning we would sleep on the concrete. My parents used a place called rent a center to

finance themselves a king-sized bed with a nice frame, a matching dresser set and a tv. They

didn't bother to get their kids anything. Rice had unlimited access to me. He often followed

me around whenever he got the opportunity. Pauline and Rice didn't allow my siblings and I

upstairs unless we were eating in the kitchen with them or mom or unless we were taking a

bath/shower. The only bathtub was upstairs. To take a bath or shower we had to have

permission. Grandma and grandpa would lock the door in the garage which was the only way

to get upstairs so we couldn't get upstairs without permission. every time I needed to take a

shower Rice knew. He would double check that the garage door was locked after I was

upstairs. He would come in while I was bathing and masturbate. I felt so repulsed and

violated. He would tell me to stop covering my body. He would say he could wait until I had to

get out. I honestly don't want to talk about this any further. It's something from which I am

still healing. I am traumatized from being repeatedly subjected to sexual abuse. Grandma was

an active hoarder. The entire house was full of these creepy porcelain dolls, carousel horses,

vases, and little bear statues. She had at least ten big curio cabinets full of them. She had

hundreds of "romance novels." They were in bags, bins and stacked on top of each other. The basement was one big room that had two little rooms in it. One of the rooms had a furnace and power box. The other room was filled with more creepy statues, old pictures, and books. I had skimmed a lot of those books. They were porn books being sold as "romance." Grandma really liked the ones with a brutish man taking a woman forcefully and then later falling for her captor. Shocking considering, she was groomed into a relationship by a 30-year-old man at 13. The garage was full of cans of food. Rice said that he needed them for the end of the world. He believed the world was at the end of times. He was bat shit crazy. My brothers and I sometimes would steal cans of food because we were so hungry. Rice would count them. When he figured out one was missing, he would get truly angry and threaten to kick us all out. Over on singular can of fruit. Grandma swore that all these things she had collected would be worth a lot of money someday. She would have garage sales and expected them to sell but they never did. Yet she kept buying more. The creek behind grandma's house kept flooding. The garage full of books and cans grew moldy. All the junk my grandma stored in the basement had grown moldy. The black mold spread to the dry walls. We started getting sick repeatedly from the mold. Grandma for a year refused to throw any of the moldy stuff away, insisting it could be saved. Everything my grandma hoarded and held onto grew moldy. It was fucking ironic. One day Mom decided she wasn't going to ask grandma anymore. She got garbage bags and started throwing everything away. This caused a huge fight. Mom and Grandma argued for hours. Mom brought the bags of moldy junk upstairs for Grandma to see. She told her if you want it so badly keep it upstairs. Grandma spent a few hours trying to scrub mold off some of the things. Eventually she gave in. The moldy junk went to the curb.

Mom told us to smash and pull the dry wall out. We didn't have gloves or masks. We just ripped apart the moldy dry wall with our bare hands. Bagged it up and to the curb it went. This didn't stop the growth of mold. The black mold was already in the ventilation system, so it had already began spreading throughout the house. The second-floor bathroom had a small leak behind the faucet that went untouched. This strain of mold mixed with the black mold from the ventilation system caused the entire bathroom to become so moldy the floor fell apart. There was no floor in the second-floor bathroom. It was completely molded away.

Grandma didn't have insurance on the house because all her bills were behind due to mom and dad mooching off her for their drugs. She didn't want to get the mold inspected because she knew the house would be condemned. Mom and dad convinced Paradise to file my siblings and me under her taxes. Since she was only seventeen, she didn't really know what tax fraud was and she wasn't allowed to even see us...so she did it. My sister claimed us on her taxes and got my parents over $10,000 back. She gave the money to our parents, and they gave her $1,000 dollars from it. The other $9,000 my parents spent on buying themselves new clothes, shoes, snacks, a $2,000 wedding ring (that they ended up pawning later), and they bought my brothers $50 good will beds so at least we didn't have to share the air mattress moms' raggedy cats kept popping. I didn't get a bed. I got to have the raggedy air mattress to myself. Oh joy. Thanks mom and dad! We didn't get new clothes, shoes or even school supplies. The other thousands of dollars they spent on painkillers, weed and alcohol. We were living off our grandma and they didn't even so much as buy groceries with the money they only received because of my siblings and me. I remember asking my parents for a singular pair of shoes they didn't even need to be new. Goodwill shoes were fine by me. They said they didn't have any money. This was 1 week after getting a $9,000 check. That same night they rented a hotel room, ordered room service, and got shit faced. While my brothers and I stayed in the basement all night waiting for them to come back. We weren't allowed to leave or go upstairs without mom and dad. Miles, who was eight, went upstairs for a snack. Rice came downstairs yelling at him. Miles has always been headstrong and confident. Without hesitation he told rice go fuck himself. Rice slapped and shoved miles down the stairs then was threatening to kill him. I panicked and called the police. I was hoping they would arrest him. I hated him. I wanted him to go to jail. To suffer for the horrible things, he did. When the police arrived, rice owned up to shoving an 8-year-old down the stairs and proceeded to argue with the police about how all these "snot nosed brats" deserve to be put in their place. The cops asked him what was wrong with him. Rice tried to swing on them. I stood in front of the house knowing I was about to get my ass whooped by my parents. Watching that piece of shit get arrested made my heart happy. It didn't last long. I was flung back into reality. Grandma was screaming for all of us to get out of her house because we ruined her life. Mom and dad were yelling at me for calling the cops. They said I should always ask before I call because things like this happen. We packed up what little clothes we had, and we loaded up into our little van. For the next week we stayed in the van in the Walmart parking lot. Finally, mom and dad said we were going to either tell paradise what happened or go to the homeless shelter. Dad said, "you'd like it if we had to go to the shelter huh woman because then you don't have to be around me or the boys" Mom started screaming at him "this isn't what I wanted this shit is your fault if you weren't so insecure, I could have kept my job". Dad turned up the radio so loud it hurt all our ears. They both proceeded to scream over the sound of "crazy train" by Ozzy Osbourne ironic, isn't it? Mom called paradise from the Walmart parking lot. We ended up staying in Paradise's boyfriends' families' garage. Their garage had been turned into a little apartment for their elderly grandma, but she had passed away, so they let us stay in it. I don't know where mom and dad went but they left the boys and I in the garage by ourselves. I saw how my sister was living with her boyfriend. I was so proud and happy for her. It was so nice compared to how we were living. I wished I could stay there forever. It sucked because I knew that the power, water, warmth, and food wouldn't last. I knew I was going to have to say goodbye to my sister and not see her for a while again. I wasn't her responsibility, but I wanted to stay with her so badly. Mom and dad came back after 3 days of being in a safe environment. They said they "found us a place." We ended up moving into dads' dealer's attic. Dad had just paid off his debt to his drug dealer Roni, so he was feeling generous. Living in Roni, the drug dealer's attic was one of the weirdest places we lived. We had to be quiet all the time. My brothers and I slept on the floor. Our parents had the only bed. We went to a new school. At first, I really enjoyed my new school. I made a lot of friends and for the first time in my life I was considered popular. People were nice to me. After a month of being at my new school rumors started floating around that this girl named Jory didn't like me. She had been making fun of my living situation. My clothes. My teeth. Which

was an easy target for people. My teeth were a big insecurity of mine. It got under my skin

right away. I started hiding my teeth when I would talk or smile. I'd cover my mouth with my

hands. I started telling the people who would tell me things about Jory that I didn't give a

fuck. Kids, especially girls instigate. Jory began mean mugging me every time we were in the

hallway and in the lunchroom. People were starting to say I was scary. Jory was a cheer

leader. She was a blonde cheerleader dating a linebacker two years older than us. She was a

preppy bitch. She was rallying people to dislike me. I was now being called scary constantly. I

started hiding in the bathroom to eat my lunch. I started dreading going to school again. It

was starting to feel just like before. I could feel tension from the second I walked in. For half

of the school year people were watching me like something was going to happen. One day

everything crumbled. I couldn't pay attention in class. I was paranoid all the time. After being

jumped for being "quiet" the thought always lingered in the back of my mind. Finally, I voiced

my concern to the school counselor. I told her I was being bullied. I was scared to even come

to school. She asked the name of the student and when I told her she called Jory out of class

for a "Sit down." A "Sit down" is a meeting where you're supposed to talk with your bully and

magically things are fixed. I was twelve so I didn't know any better. Jory came into the

counselor's room and sat down. She had a huge smirk on her face. She thought this was so

funny. The counselor told me to "Tell Jory how I feel." I was so embarrassed. I said I felt like

Jory was a bully and that I didn't understand what I did to her. Jory apologized. None of it was genuine yet the counselor said, "Well that's all the time I have for today girls hug it out and get back to class." We exchanged a hug. Not even an hour later when I was walking in the hallway people were laughing at me. Jory told everyone "I snitched because I was scary." It wasn't even two days later I went to my locker in between class to grab my books and who's in front of my locker? Jory and she's making out with her boyfriend. Her locker was nowhere near mine. She was Frenching her boyfriend in front of my locker to make me late for class. "Can you move" I asked nicely. Jory shoved me and said, "Fuck you snitch" and went back to kissing her boyfriend. I yanked Jory down by her blonde ponytail to the ground and just started punching her in the face. Over, over, over, and over. She was scratching, screaming, and pulling my hair. "Get off of me" then when I saw red from her nose, I started swinging harder. She was flailing all around. She ended up turning herself head down to the floor. I was sitting on top of her just punching the sides of her face. She screamed like nothing I've ever heard in my entire life. The best way I could describe it is a baby pig squealing. There was a crowd of people around us. phones out. some yelling 'FAYE whoop her ass" some telling Jory to "get up." Out of nowhere Jory's boyfriend shoved me so hard I flew off her and into a garbage can. Still in a blind fit of rage I got up and ran as fast as I could towards Jory's boyfriend and shoved him with all my 120 pounds of bodyweight. He was a shit linebacker. He was always benched for a reason. He fell backwards and hit his head on the lock of a locker. Jory had halfway rolled over and started to stand up, but she was wobbly. I ran at her swinging. I put up with this bitch for half of the school year picking at me. I hid in the bathroom during lunch. I ducked my head. I kept my mouth closed. I tried to talk it out. I did all the right things to avoid it. She wanted this. All the anger built up. It took three school security guards to pull me off Jory. I was swinging on all of them. I punched two of the guards and elbowed the third. As the security guards picked me up and pulled me away her, I had a death grip on her hair. A huge chunk ripped out. I swung the hair over my head and yelled "who's scary now bitch?" I was fighting the security guards with all my might. Unable to calm down. I felt the school had failed me. They let me get bullied. I was handcuffed in the middle school office to a chair that was welded to the floor and not only did they handcuff my wrists but also my feet. I was only twelve. As I sat there in handcuffs, I screamed about how it's illegal. They shouldn't even have handcuffs. I just wanted to go home. Jory's mom came into the office. In front of two of the principals and all three of the receptionists. This grown woman was threatening to beat me up and she spit in my face. None of the other adults in the room did anything. No one stopped her and if she had slapped or punched me, I am fully confident they wouldn't have done anything to defend me. When my mom and dad got to the school, they uncuffed me when my mom said it was illegal as fuck for a school to handcuff a 12-year-old who's been bullied for half of the school year. One of the few times in my life has my mom ever stood up for me. This was one of those times. Jory's mom was fucking one of the principals and the other one was her uncle. Jory got away with everything she did because she had privileges I didn't. I was expelled that day and Jory didn't even get suspended. Everything was on camera. Jory's boyfriend didn't receive punishment either because he was on the football team. I was told to gather my things from my locker and leave the property. I would be going to "Fresh start." The school for bad kids. I cleared my locker and exited out the side door where my bus usually was. My parents didn't know which side because they never took me to school or picked me up. They were on the wrong side of the school. The second I stepped outside I heard someone yelling at me. It's Jory and her bitch mom. They're in the hospital parking lot. Jory's mom is telling me to come over to them for a rematch. This old bitch really thinks I'm dumb enough to go over there like they aren't going to jump me. Jory was making fun of my teeth. I said "that's why I fucked your face up" over and over. She was salty. If she really wanted a rematch the bitch could have walked over without her mommy. She didn't want a fair one. She had a fat goose egg under her eye and welts all over her face. Jory's mom started walking across the parking lot towards me with Jory right as my parents figured out, they were on the wrong side of the building. My mom who is over three hundred pounds steps out of the car. "what's up bitch?" I started walking towards Jory and her mom with my mom. It's about to be a family affair. Jory and her scary ass mom backed up and got into their vehicle. If they couldn't jump me, they didn't want to fight. It wasn't hard to tell where Jory got her personality. Her bitch mom was a bully just like her daughter. I was expelled. Jory wasn't cause her mom was a walking condom. I was really starting to hate school. It was just another system that failed me.

Chapter 7
Always
watching.

Over the break I started hanging out with an old friend from Elementary school Casey. Casey and I hadn't seen each other or been close since kindergarten. She wasn't a good influence. She smoked cigarettes, drank, smoked weed and hung out with boys. She was so cool. She always had dyed hair and cute clothes. We spent our time watching movies, smoking cigarettes, and drinking whenever we could get our hands on a bottle. I never actually inhaled the cigarettes. I just pretended to look cool so Casey would want to hang out with me. She wasn't close to her mom and dad either. Casey's mom was a real piece of shit. We had a lot in common. We came from broken homes. We both were labeled "bad kids." We spent time together pretty much every day. I'd rather be with her than getting my ass whooped by my parents. I was a bad friend. I used Casey as an escape. Although she had her vices. No one deserves to be used out of fear or boredom. Casey was a good person. She has a beautiful kind heart. She has always been that way. She wanted to go to the beach. We got all cute. Took some pre walk selfies then we walked to the beach. It was about an hour's walk. We laughed and told stories the entire time. We spent all day at the beach. Swimming in the river. Tanning. We had so much fun. We walked back to her grandma's house. Within an hour of being at her grandma's house her blackberry phone rings. She answers. It was someone talking in "the scream" voice asking if we liked scary movies. I just assumed it was one of the boys she was messing around with messing with her until my phone rang. I had a track phone. No one except mom, dad and Casey had my number. I answered and the man on the phone said, "I can see you" he snickered "I'm always watching." Still thinking it's a prank I jokingly

asked, "What are we wearing?"

"Red top, black and white shorts with fuzzy white socks" I dropped the phone and started

screaming at Casey.

"He is watching us!"

The curtains in Casey's room were open. We closed them and calmed ourselves.

"It was probably one of the neighbor boys" Casey said.

We were alone in the house. Casey's grandma wasn't coming home for another hour. It was

just a boy playing a prank. I hoped. We moved from Casey's room to the living room. We

decided to color to calm ourselves and watch a movie. Both of our phones kept getting text

messages. They were coming in so quickly. Different numbers from every text message but

they all had the same signature "always watching." The text messages kept getting worse. The

man was saying he was going to kick down the door and kill us. He went into detail about how

he was going to tie us down and rape us. Force us to have children and then cut us up into little pieces and feed us to them. The messages kept getting increasingly disturbed. When

Casey's grandma came home, we were crying and showed her all the messages. She started

telling Casey it was her fault for always messing around with boys. Casey's grandma was

holding the phone and another text popped up.

"Hi grandma come outside to play."

There was no way the person texting could have known Casey's grandma just had gotten

home unless he really was watching. We called the police. The text messages halted. We

showed the cops. They walked around the house. There were large shoe impression marks

outside of the living room window and Casey's bedroom window. The cops said it must be a

boy playing a prank. "Boys will be boys." The second the officers left the text messages

resumed. Threat after threat. detailing murdering us. The messages on my phone were more

disturbing than on Casey's. He kept saying "come outside to play." I freaked out. I called my

parents to get me. Of course, they were mad at me. Blamed me for the situation. "I must have

done something." "This is why we don't want you hanging out with Casey." When I got home the texts didn't stop. My mom took my track phone and started reading the messages. She

was disturbed. She called the police again. They took a report but said they couldn't do

anything because the numbers weren't real. They didn't take it seriously. I was a 13-year-old

girl being threatened to be kidnapped and brutally murdered in detail, but they couldn't care

less. I had over 1,000 texts in 2 days. Mom started getting messages. The house phone started

getting calls. When mom answered it would just be breathing. Loud breathing. Sometimes the

man on the phone would just say "always watching" over and over. Mom took and kept my

track phone. One night I was sleeping, and I woke up because I heard a strange noise. I had

this horrible feeling. I rolled over in bed. I didn't have curtains or blinds in my room. There was

a man with his hand on my window just staring at me. I screamed loudly. Frozen in fear. My

parents came running into the room. "He's here he was at the window" I shrieked. Mom and

dad called the police. They just seemed annoyed. They didn't even want to go look around

because it was storming outside. Reluctantly they looked at my window and saw big boot

imprints right at my window and the dust on my window had a hand shaped imprint. They took pictures and said there wasn't much else they could do but to make sure everything was

locked up and sit a squad car outside our house for the night. They kept asking what he

looked like. If I got a "good look at him." He had something on his face. A mask. I think. I don't

know. I was so scared it's not like I was trying to memorize everything. I had been woken out

of my sleep. I knew he was white from the mouth and eye holes in the mask. I knew he was

very tall. That was it. If it weren't for the massive footprints leading to and away from my

window, I doubt they would have believed me. The cops treated me like I was fucking nuts.

Things were quiet for a while. I decided to stay away from Casey. Maybe it was her fault.

Maybe it was some creepy guy she met on Omegal. Casey regularly would video chat strange

men on Omegal chat. It was mostly perverts. I didn't want to rule anything out. I had other

things I needed to focus on. We were moving out of the drug dealer's attic to move into

mom's cousin's basement. I was starting my new school after being expelled. 3 months of

"Fresh start" then I was sent to an uppity new school. People wore Hollister and brand-new

cowboy boots. We were freshman and some of them drove cars their mommies and daddies bought them to school. It was that type of school. I didn't fit in at all. I was extremely poor. I was technically homeless; we were living in my mom's cousin's basement. I slept on the concrete floor with a pillow and a sheet. Sharing the basement room with mom, dad, Dean, Miles, and Melvan. Mom told me I wouldn't have to walk to school anymore. I'll get a school bus now. Within 2 weeks of attending my new school, a girl named Moon decided she didn't like me. Here the fuck we go again. Three for three. It started with dirty looks then it escalated to other girls telling me "She said this." I was at the point in my life where I was so tired of being bullied. I knew how quickly things can get out of hand with bullies from my last two schools. After a few months of living in my mom's cousin's basement things went south. Mom and dad were supposed to be paying him money for us to stay but of course they bought Norco's and Oxy's instead. Cousin Randy legally got an eviction notice without telling our parents. One day when I got home from school the police were there and told us to get our stuff and get out. I grabbed what little clothes I had and put them in a trash bag. We ended up staying in a homeless shelter. Dad didn't like that the homeless shelter kept men and women separate so we slept in the Walmart parking lot in our van. It was hot and miserable. We had to pee in a water bottle, poop in a bag, or drive to McDonald's to use the

public restroom. Dad only did that for mom. If you didn't have to go when we were there it

was a bottle or bag for you. 2 weeks after this we were living in a travel inn motel. My

brothers and I slept on the floor as usual sharing one sheet between us while mom and dad

slept on the only bed. We went to the food pantry for food. We only ate things out of a can.

Mom entered us in a special program for homeless kids which helped her get food stamps,

housing, and transportation for us. Now instead of taking a normal school bus to school I had

a small white van that picked me and the other homeless kids up to drop us off at school.

Moon didn't waste any time making fun of me for being homeless. Calling me dirty, poor and

a peasant. I waited until gym class for my opportunity. Bitch you got me fucked up. The gym

teacher announced we were playing dodgeball. I made sure I picked to be on the opposite

side as moon. I will admit I was throwing the dodgeball as hard as I could. I ousted at least

nine people myself. It came down to just moon and I. What great luck. At the end of

dodgeball there's no sides to the court. I started chasing her in front of the entire class with a

dodgeball. I threw it as hard as I could at the back of her head. She fell face first in front of the entire class. I was sent to the principal's office. I didn't care because I felt like Moon would

leave me alone after being embarrassed like that. I was wrong. I got suspended for 3 days. I

came back the next week to school only to immediately be rushed by a bunch of girls.

Everyone was telling me moon said, "Faye was so scared of me that she dropped out." They

said Moon said she was going to "beat my ass on sight." I only asked one question. "Who's her

first hour class?" A huge crowd followed me as I walked to Moons first hour. The adrenaline

was pumping as I got closer to her classroom. Moon was sitting at her desk. I walked in. I told

her to get up. We walked to the hallway, and we started fighting. It honestly wasn't much of a

fight she grabbed my hair but physically she was so weak. Within two punches I put her on her

ass and sat on top of her punching her. Moon was the weakest person I'd fought. She had no

physical strength or fighting skills. Moon's first hour English teacher tried to grab me off her.

Instinctually being grabbed I elbowed backwards hitting him in the nose. I wasn't thinking of

anything other than every time I got bullied. Every time I felt embarrassed. Every time I hid in

the bathroom at lunch. Every time I avoided doing normal things because I did feel scared. I

wasn't scared anymore. At one point I was slamming her head against the floor. There was a huge crowd of students around us. Screams of thrills and horror. The two official school security guards tackled me hard to the ground and dragged me to the office where an actual officer later came, and I was placed under arrest. I was cuffed, read my rights, and brought to the juvenile detention center. I finally calmed down. I realized I went too far. Moon wasn't sitting in juvey. I was. It didn't matter that moon said she was going to whoop my ass because she didn't. I went to her class. I instigated that moment. Did she deserve it? Hell yeah. Should I have done it? Probably not. The police made me sit on a very thin bench. They threatened to pepper spray me if I moved off the bench. The bench was so thin no joke I couldn't even fit one ass cheek on it, and I was tiny. It hurt to sit on the bench, eventually I sat on the floor. I told the cop "Just pepper spray me I don't care my parents are going to do worse anyways."

They laughed. I wasn't joking. Eventually mom and Paradise showed up to get me. I started crying immediately. I didn't even want to fight Moon. I just was so scared of things getting out of hand. I got jumped with railroad rocks. I let Jory bully me for half of the school year. Then she and her boyfriend fought me for going to my own locker. I was so afraid that if I didn't stand up for myself, I'd get bullied or jumped again. The anger and anxiety I felt was unbearable. Mom said, "I can't believe you; your father is going to deal with you." He did. He

made me go outside the motel. I picked a switch, and he whooped my ass until I couldn't

stand. He was swinging so hard he was missing my ass and hitting my back. I couldn't sit or

stand up straight for a few days. I was expelled from a second school. I was ruining my own

opportunities. I wasn't getting an education. I was far behind my peers. I had crippling anxiety.

I presented as a hard ass because I couldn't show how scared I was. I couldn't let anyone bully

me anymore. I couldn't do anything right. I had nobody in my corner. No one was coming to

look for me. My dad kept making comments like "I brought you into this world and I can take

you out." I thought often they'll kill me and just keep collecting the free state money and food

stamps. It's not like anyone would know. I wouldn't even fight back if they did. I was so

depressed. I had no space because we lived in such close quarters. The only place I had any

kind of privacy was the bathroom. I started staring at myself for lengthy periods of time in the

bathroom. Picking myself apart. I got bullied because of my hair, my fucked-up teeth, my

body. It was me. I was the problem. I tried filing my teeth with a nail file. It hurt so bad to eat

or drink. My teeth were so sensitive to hot and cold. I broke apart my mom's razor. I cut the vein right above my elbow. The first time I cut I wanted to kill myself. I didn't realize it would

burn so much. I didn't realize it would bleed so much. I didn't have the guts to keep cutting as

hard as I knew it would take. It hurt so much. I wrapped my arm up. I wore long sleeves to

hide what I'd done. I started cutting regularly but I moved to cutting the inside of my thighs. I

didn't want to have to answer any questions. It was a rush of pain. It stung. Then the

adrenaline would kick in to numb the pain. Just another way I was fucked up. I didn't have any

hope at this point. I didn't have any friends. I didn't even feel close to the siblings I lived with.

We were always arguing with each other because we had no space, no privacy and had to

share everything. It was exhausting. I felt invisible. I can't say how my siblings felt but I'm sure

they felt like shit too. I was on my own pity party. All I could think about was myself. After a

year of living in one room in the travel inn motel our parents told us that the special homeless

program had gotten us a house. They just had to pay $300 a month. Reduced rent if they

followed the rules. We lived in this rickety old blue house. For the first time in years, I had my

own room. I was so happy. I didn't mind sleeping on the floor. I had always slept on the floor

but at least now I had my own space to do it. My room even had a bathroom attached to it and a big closet. I didn't have any clothes, but I would imagine hanging them up artfully

arranged if I did. I felt hopeful. Dad wasn't drinking. He was sick. He had liver failure from HEP

C. He was approved for a dangerous trial drug to cure him. His lungs and liver were failing. He

only took his pain pills and his trial drug. He was working even though he was sick. Since he

was making so much money working the reduced rent was removed. Mom didn't slow down

on her pill popping and weed smoking even though dad was sober. She didn't care that he

risked relapsing with the constant temptation. She only cared about being so high she could

sleep all day. It financially drained dad. It got prioritized overpaying rent. Within 3 months of

being in the new house we were homeless again. Mom and dad said we had a new house into

which we were moving. Mom was so excited to announce the new house was right across the

street from grandma and grandpa. I almost threw up. I knew that meant nothing good for me.

Chapter 8

RUNAWAY.

With everything happening in my life it's important not to forget there was never any extended period I was free from my grandfather. Throughout every point from as young as I can remember my grandfather molested and raped me every chance he got. There were brief periods of time where I wasn't forced to go to their house to "help" with the paper route.

Sometimes the abuse with mom and dad was so bad I wanted to go to grandma and grandpas.

Sometimes the physical abuse from Dad was too much. No one unless they've been in my shoes gets to judge me. Mom used to say because I wanted to go to their house that grandpa must not have been so bad. Mom had never gotten beaten by dad with a belt buckle or a switch. She had, however, been choked and slapped by dad. She forgot how much it hurt.

How scared it made you feel. It's because she just didn't have sympathy for me. At the very least I thought she'd understand. Plus, Grandma always gave me clean clothes, food, a hot bath, and a bed to sleep in even though she didn't like me. A few weeks before we moved into the new house something big had happened. On the paper route Grandpa rice pulled down a road I didn't recognize. I was 2 am and pitch-black outside. I knew what he was going to do.

He parked the car. He got out in the backseat where I was. He started touching me. "Don't fight it" he said in my ear. I punched him as hard as I could and shoved him away from me. He

had this crazed look in his eyes. I thought for sure he was going to kill me. Fight or flight kicked

in. I was fully prepared to fight. I was done being a victim. He got back in the car. We

continued the paper route like nothing happened. He didn't say a word to me. That was the

last time I went on the paper route. I refused to go after that. Rice didn't pressure mom into

making me go either. I didn't like the new house. It was too close to their house. I had Sex ed

at school last year. I knew that I was not "playing games." Since I was five years old, I was being

sexually assaulted. My grandfather was manipulating me into making me think it was normal

when it wasn't. I felt disgusted. I felt dirty. I couldn't sleep. I stopped eating. I started talking

back more to my parents. I started cussing teachers out in school and walking out. I had such

a temper. All I could feel was anger or pain. No one noticed any of my pain only my anger. I

was always the problem, it never mattered what anyone did to me just how I reacted. We

lived in the new house for about 3 months. One day mom said, "kids pack up we're being

evicted again because we couldn't afford it." I snapped. "couldn't or wouldn't?" Dad and mom at the same time said, "excuse me little girl who the fuck do you think you're talking to." I

confidently said, "I'M TIRED OF THIS SHIT." Dad hopped up off the sofa and grabbed me by my

face. He pinned me against the wall "shut the fuck up little girl" he said through gritted teeth. I

held my ground. I didn't drop my angry face for a second. I shoved his arm. He dropped me. I

just melted into a little puddle on the ground. I knew they picked this house for a reason. They

never had any fucking intentions of keeping up with the rent. They were going to move us

back into my grandparent's basement. Mom liked living in grandmas because she could spend

every fucking dollar on getting high. All she cared about was being high. I decided I would try

one last time with my parents. I wrote a note. "Mom, I can't move in with grandma and

grandpa. Grandpa is a pedophile, and I can't eat or sleep. I don't feel safe. I don't want to play

grandpa's games anymore. I don't want to be raped or touched. I am not moving into their

house no matter what." I gave mom the note and I was crying so hard I was hyperventilating. I

couldn't do it anymore. This was my breaking point. Mom reads the note. She calls Paradise in

her room and closes the door. My room was right next to mom's. I could hear them talking loudly. Mom said "She's just doing it for attention, she always does this shit. She just doesn't want us to be happy. She wants us to be homeless." I didn't stay to listen to anything else. I heard what I needed to. I was done. Fuck everybody. I walked out of the door with nothing. No phone, no clothes, no money. I walked to Casey's. When I got to Casey's she was spending time together with a boy named Key. We had spent time together with Key before. I knew he had a girlfriend. Keys girlfriend Becky was nice. I didn't like that Casey was kissing Key knowing he had a girlfriend. I told Casey what happened with my parents. She knew about my grandfather. She was one of the only friends I ever confided in. Within 20 minutes of me getting to Casey's house the police showed up looking for me. Mom didn't waste any time calling to report me as a runaway. I was scrambling to find a place to hide. I crawled in Casey's dryer. I pulled her clothes over myself hoping they wouldn't find me. I watched through the dryer as the police tore Casey's room apart. They pulled out all her dresser drawers. Knocked her stuff over. Pulled her bed off the frame, left it on the floor. They completely trashed Casey's room then left. Casey said, "they're gone but you got to go just walk to Key's." I knew

Keys house was about 15 minutes away. I walked with Casey to his house. Crying my eyes out.

When I got there Becky was there. Becky and Casey exchanged words. Becky didn't like Casey

because she knew there was something going on with Key. It was the first time we talked. She

didn't know what I was going through, but she was nice to me. Bad knowing Key was kissing

Casey. I told Becky and I left keys. I hitchhiked rides all night until I got to a public library in

Michigan two states away. I logged onto Facebook. I hit up mom's sister who I knew didn't

really like mom or dad. I begged her to please get me. I told her I was scared and didn't have

anywhere to go. She got me. I stayed at her house for a week until Paradise messaged me

begging me to come back. Paradise told me I could come live with her. She would take care of

me and protect me. I told paradise where I was. Mom and dad along with the police showed

up. The police started lecturing me as if they knew shit. If only they knew they were helping

abusers. They didn't care what I had to say. They told me the next time I ran away I would go

to the juvenile detention center and then a foster home. As soon as we got in the car mom and

dad started telling me how stupid, selfish, and disgusting I am. "I hope you're proud of yourself little girl." I didn't say anything to them. I knew when we got back to grandmas, I was running

away again only this time I wouldn't make the same mistakes. Only we didn't pull up to

grandmas. We pulled up to Paradise's boyfriend's families' house. I got out of the car

confused. Paradise had a huge smile on her face. I started crying. She didn't betray me. She

was saving me. She didn't believe mom. She pretended so she could save me. Paradises family

took me in with open arms. They let me stay in their home. I felt so blessed. For the first time

in years, I had hope. I got three meals a day. I had a safe place to lay my head. I had a soft bed.

Clean clothes. No threat of danger. I could be a normal 13-year-old. Paradise and her boyfriend

Landon felt like more of a mom and dad than my own. Paradise bought me clothes. She also

gave me her old ones. Landon's mom Sammy was very welcoming. She hugged me. As she held

me, I cried because even though I hated my parents, it was hurtful my parents abandoned me

when I wouldn't move into my rapist's home. Sammy already didn't like Mom and dad from

everything Paradise had told them. She was a good mom. She loved her kids. She felt sorry for

me. She felt sorry for my brothers we couldn't help too. Sammy helped Paradise enroll me in

school. Paradise and Landon worked together. They always made sure I had a ride to school.

After about 4 months Paradise and Landon moved out of Sammy's house. We moved into their

own townhouse. I got my own bedroom. I went to a new school. I was nervous because it was

another uppity school. I wondered if I'd fit in. On the first day I wore a brown tracksuit with

golden sequins on the side. When I walked in everyone stared at me. This was a ridiculously

small town. Everyone knew everyone. So, nobody knew me, but everyone talked about me. I

became kind of popular. I couldn't tell if it was because I was new or because people liked my

confidence. On my first day the boys I was sitting next to right in front of me started arguing

about who got to sit next to me to talk to me. I didn't like either of them. I made a lot of

friends. I made sure to be nice to everyone. I wasn't shy in telling people to shut the fuck up

either. I wouldn't bite my tongue. I didn't care if I got in trouble because I wasn't in threat of

getting beaten at home. Some of the preppy girls didn't like me. It was their own insecurities. I

didn't do anything to them. They didn't like me because I was the shiny new thing that took

away their attention. Sorry you bitches were basic and boring. Those same preppy girls who

prided themselves on making fun of me for being different peaked in high school. It never

changed. I never got an apology, and I didn't deserve to be picked at. Honestly, they're lucky I didn't beat them up. The preppy girls would never say anything to my face. There was only one preppy girl who had some balls. It all started when this one boy Reenon started talking to me. Reenon before meeting me was dating a beautiful preppy cheerleader named Adrienne. They dated on and off for like 2 years. She hated me. I didn't know their history when I came to a new school. If I had I never would have even bothered talking to the guy. So, I had no idea why she was giving me death stares and whispering to her friends about me. It was starting to piss me off. One day I the hallway and I gave her the finger. "Fuck you bitch." One of my friends in Spanish class Thomas told me that she didn't like me because she had history with Reenon. I asked Reenon about it. He said they had been broken up for a long time. That wasn't true but I didn't know anything different from what he told me. He said she was just "a bitter ex." If I were smarter, I would have walked away from the situation. Reenon and I started dating. Behind my back he was still talking to and seeing Adrienne. Reenon and I only dated for about 2 weeks. He was a horrible person. He only dated me to try and tell all the boys at our school we fucked. We didn't. What he did to me was beyond fucked up. I'm not keeping his secrets because his dad is the news anchor. I don't give a fuck. My neighbor friend

Alexi had a house party. I had one beer which Reenon gave me. I started feeling strange and

tired. I was nodding in and out. The last thing I remember was my "Friends" crystal, Mandy

and Tye leaving me in the upstairs room to sleep. When I woke up, I immediately had to

throw up. I was so sore. I had blood trickling down my leg on my white leggings. Reenon was

next to me on the ground. I asked crystal, Mandy and ty what happened, and they said "oh

Reenon fingered you." They knew I was unconscious. Yet they left me up there with him. He

was violent because there was blood and extreme soreness. I was so embarrassed. I thought I
had gotten drunk off one beer and done something to provoke that. I don't really know why I
made excuses for him. I guess it's because I get attached quickly. I love hard. When I like
someone, I really like them. I liked Reenon. I was extremely attached to him. The next day

when Reenon was at my house when we were on the sofa, he kissed me and tried to push my

head towards him to give him head. I told him no and to leave. He dumped me over text, and I

cried and cried and had a complete meltdown. I didn't even know why I was so upset. He was

a douchebag. Being rejected by a loser like that really struck a nerve. A few years ago, for the

first time in my life I confronted him about sexually assaulting me. He apologized. He knew what he had done. I kept the screenshots. I always keep receipts. Fuck you. I don't give a shit if you're sorry. If you were sorry, you would have taken accountability, then. You didn't. You took accountability when I called you out as a grown woman with a large enough following on social media to ruin your life. I spiraled out of control. I started hanging out with other friends who partied all the time. I just wanted to be numb. I ended up getting myself into another situation. At 16 my friend Melany invited me and Maritza over to her house for a little kickback. She was dating an older guy who had an even older guy as a roommate. He was thirty. The roommate roofied Maritza and me. I remember I laid down on the sofa because my whole body felt limp. The next thing I remember is this 30-year-old man picking me up. He had to physically carry me to his room. I couldn't even move my body to fight him off. I kept saying no. Trying to shove him, but my limbs were so limp. He raped both of us. His name was Santi. Things just kept getting worse. Landon was cheating on paradise, and they ended up breaking up. That meant I didn't have anywhere else to go. I had to move back in with my parents or go to foster care.

CHAPTER 9

SPIRALING.

After everything that happened. I was forced to move back in with mom and dad. They were

still living in grandma's basement. Neither of them had jobs. It was different though. Rice had

dementia. He was forgetting everything. It had started with keys. It advanced to places then

people. He didn't know who I was. He forgot what he did. I hated him even more. Why did

this piece of shit get to forget what he'd done but I have to live with it for the rest of my life?

Everyone pitied him. They helped him. I was so angry. He forgot while I suffered with it. It was

torture. Grandma wouldn't get off my back. Always saying I was disrespectful to Rice because I

refused to call him grandpa. I refused to bring him food. I wouldn't help him if he wandered

out of the house. I wouldn't chase him. He was lucky I even told mom when he wandered off.

I wished he'd wander into traffic. I only told mom because I knew she'd have dad beat me

later for not telling her. I learned that lesson the hard way. Mom and dad's drug addiction was

the worst it had ever been. They kept scheming for ways to get money. They stole jewelry

from grandma. Pawned everything they could. Took out loans, even old ALL of our monthly food stamps. Mom got so desperate when she'd get food from the food pantry, she'd stand in

front of grocery stores offering all of it to people for a small price. My brothers and I were so

hungry all the time. We were only guaranteed food at school. Many days we went without

having anything to eat. The feeling of starvation isn't something I'd wish on my worst enemy.

When tax season came around mom and dad had a big plan to keep steady income. They

committed tax fraud frequently. They would find some sucker to claim Dean, Miles, Melvan,

and I on their taxes. Mom and Dad would pay the person hush money and keep the other

$10,000. Yeah, you read that right $10,000. This was the regular going rate for four children

under the age of eighteen. Give or take 2,500 per kid. Some years it was more. Instead of

getting us a place to live, beds, clothes or food mom and dad spent it on themselves as usual.

They bought pills, weed and alcohol and ate out at steak houses like we weren't all living in a

basement. Then they decided to use $4,000 on weed grow supplies. They started illegally

growing weed in grandma's basement. Grandma was against drugs and alcohol. She was

working at a local grocery store and paying all the bills. Rice's disability was barely enough to

pay his own medical bills. Grandma was making arrangements on every bill. Water, electric, gas, mortgage. Everyday grandma gave mom $40-$60 to go to the store to feed everyone.

Every single day. Let's do some quick math 40x7=280 and 60x7=420. That was my grandma's

entire check at the grocery store. Mom didn't get food. She would buy Rice and grandma tv

dinners that were $1, get spaghetti or hot dogs. She spent the rest of the money on Norco's,

Oxy's, weed or alcohol. Mom and dad spent 90% of their days so high, they wouldn't move

out of bed. Grandma started catching on to the fact that the money didn't match the food

mom was bringing home. She started getting more frustrated. Grandma knew mom was lying.

Mom needed grandma. Grandma needed mom. It was a parasitic relationship. Grandma

couldn't kick Mom out because that would leave Rice home alone. He would wander off.

Grandma didn't have health insurance. She couldn't afford a care giver. Mom needed grandma

for a place to live and drug money. I applied for my workers permit at 15. I was approved. I

got my first job at Chuck e cheese. Within the first week of working there, a girl named Anna

had decided she didn't like me. I tried to move forward from it. I tried to ignore her mean

mugging me. Whispering about me. Picking at me. Rallying the other simple-minded girls

against me. It turned into that he said she said bullshit. Where people come and tell you terrible things someone else allegedly said about you because they didn't have the balls to say it directly to you. I didn't care. I needed this job. If it wasn't for that bitch, I genuinely enjoyed it. Not the chuck e costume though. It smelled like throw up and farts. It was also hot as hell.

Dancing around in a giant rat costume made the kids go crazy. I enjoyed watching kids be kids. Having the childhood, I wished I had. It was a cake job. Mom and dad confiscated all my money, but they were a lot nicer to me because I was providing for them. It made things easier to get less physical and verbal daily degradation. Key's ex-girlfriend Becki asked for a reference to start working with me at chuck e cheese. I begged the manager to hire my friend.

A week after Becki started things escalated with Anna. Anna would do coke in the back room with the other girls. One day she got hyped up. I went to clock out for my lunch break. Anna had half of the floor mopped. I stepped on the floor to go to the clock out clock. What was I supposed to do levitate over it? Anna got in my face. Clapping and yelling loudly. Something about beating my ass. If I'm being honest... I don't remember what she said. I was fighting the invasive thoughts in my head to not punch her in her tobacco-stained teeth right then and there. She kept talking and throwing her hands near my face. I looked her up and down. All I said was "I'm off at 11. I'll meet you out front." Everyone heard what I said. Everyone was going "OOOOOOOOO." Getting hyped to watch a fight. One of the boys, James, we worked with knew who I was because he went to one of the schools I got kicked out of. James told Anna not to fight me because she would lose. I waited out front at 11. Anna snuck out the back. No show. Scary bitch. The next day a girl named Reesa I'd never met before is messaging me on Facebook talking crazy shit. Reesa worked at chuck e cheese. It was her second day. Again, we'd never met. She wasn't very bright. She said she's going to beat my ass for talking about her baby cousins. She says she's going to be at my house in 10 minutes. Be ready to fight. I threw my hair up. Put my sneakers on. I told mom and dad I was stepping out to fight a bitch up because she's pulling up to the house. They were mad telling me not to. I told them If she comes here, I'm whooping her ass. I told them truthfully; I had no idea who this girl was. I showed mom the messages. She nodded. She knew at that moment I was throwing hands regardless of what she told me to do. Ol 'girl pulled up. Brave and stupid I give her props. I could have shot her or jumped her. Mom, dad, and Miles came outside with me. Miles just wanted to watch me fight. Reesa had her mom with two small children that I'd assume were her baby cousins and one of our coworkers who was her girlfriend, Dee. I recognized Dee as one of Anna's minions. The second I saw Anna's minion I knew they set Reesa up. I tried talking to the girl. I told her" I've never met you. How would I talk about your baby cousins? Who told you I said that." Reesa wasn't trying to listen. She wasn't very smart. We squared up. Fair fight. We both ran up to each other and started swinging. I ended up on top of Reesa. She had a death grip on my hair. She was scratching my neck with one hand and pulling my hair with the other. I was swinging. Left, right, left, left, right. She wouldn't let go of my hair, so I ended up on top of her. We squabbled on the ground. She ended up face first to the dirt as I sat on her punching the back of her head and side of her face. She let go of my hair. She put her hands up attempting to block my hits. I don't know how long I was swinging on her. I was fucking her up. She started making this God-awful scream and saying, "get the fuck off of me." She grabbed back onto my hair again. I told her "Let go of my hair." She let go. We both stood up. She was out of breath but said" Round two." I was fucking tired. We both ran back up to each other but instead of grabbing my hair she grabs my shirt trying to pull it over my head so

I can't see. I grabbed a fist full of her hair and swung her whole body over sideways. For a

second, we were both kicking at each other. I got one good kick in her face and was able to

regain control. I was back sitting on top of her just like before. She was face first in the dirt

trying to guard the sides of her face with her hands. Out of nowhere something knocks me off

her for a second. I didn't know what it was. I'm focused on Reesa. I heard off to the side

someone saying, "no I'm a girl, I'm a girl." While I was fighting Reesa Dee punched me in the

side of the head to knock me off her girlfriend. Miles punched Dee in the face. He thought Dee

was a boy. Miles punched some brain power into that bitch because she quickly said she

wasn't getting involved again. I'm still sitting on top of Reesa fucking her up. Again WHAP.

Something knocked me on the side of the head so hard it knocked me halfway off Reesa. With

the adrenaline pumping I didn't feel it. I just knew something big had smacked me. I heard

mom and Reesa's mom fighting. Reesa's mom pulled out a belt. She knocked me in the head

with the buckle cause her punk ass daughter couldn't fight for shit. Mom put Reesa's mom in a

chokehold. Reesa's mom was swimming for air. Reesa's mom started yelling for the baby cousins to call 911. I told Reesa's dumb ass I didn't even want to fight. I didn't know her. Reesa

isn't saying anything. I'm still swinging on the back of her head. She's going in and out of

consciousness. Dad pulled me off Reesa by my shirt. As he's dragging me away from her, I'm

kicking her in the face as hard as I can. Dad keeps saying "YOU'RE DONE. YOU'RE DONE." I

wasn't done. I was mad. I'm tired of bitches trying me for no reason. She wanted to fight. I gave

her the fight of a lifetime. She will never forget that ass whooping. The police pulled up. Reesa's

face is fucked up. She looked like she got run over by a bus. She's bleeding. She's got fat ass

goose eggs all over her face. I'd never fucked a girl up like Reesa. My hair was raggedy from

getting pulled, I had scratch marks on my neck and small cut above my eyebrow from Reesa's

mom's belt buckle. I was unscathed compared to Reesa. The police said even though the fight

was on my property since I fucked Reesa up so bad that if one of us pressed charges, we were

both going to have to fight it in court. I told the officer "I'm cool, I don't want to press

charges." I was proud of myself. This pissed the officer off. "You should both be ashamed. You

should start acting like ladies." Blahblahblah. He didn't know our story. He just knew I fucked

that bitch up. Reesa and her posse left. The next day Reesa quit chuck e cheese. Dee was silent. Anna had a brand-new attitude. She avoided me. She knew I would dog walk her. She

knew I knew she sent Reesa to my house. I ended up calling chuck e cheese corporate. I

snitched that Anna, and her minions did coke in the back room. I snitched that the manager

would buy alcohol and cigarettes for the minors. This ended up getting me fired. Becky was

now being harassed by Anna. The next day after I snitched Anna went up to Becky and

slammed her head against a hand sanitizer dispenser. She then proceeded to windmill Becky

with two of her minions also swinging on Becky. A third minion recorded it and posted it on

Facebook. All because Becky was friends with me. Where was Anna's energy to do that to me?

Anna and her sad little gang were proud of themselves for jumping her. Becky came to my

house crying. She told me what happened. I tied my hair up. Laced my shoes up. We walked

back to chuck e cheese for a fair fight. Anna's scary ass hid behind the police who informed us

we were banned from the property. Stepping foot on it again meant we would be trespassing

and go to jail. Becky, her friend Zafree and I were driving around chilling a week later with the

windows down. Out of nowhere a cold soda hits the side of my face. Anna's scary whore ass threw a soda on me from the backseat of some dude's car. They sped off thinking shit was sweet. If she was brave, she would have gotten out to fight me. We were chasing them at high speed. They pulled into the chuck e cheese parking lot. Becky wouldn't stop the car. I yelled for her to stop. I opened the car door. I was so angry I jumped out thinking I was going to land on my feet. I obviously ate shit. I tumbled over because she was going thirty-five mph.

I got up and started running towards their vehicle in the parking lot. Bitch I'm going to fuck you up. Sending bitches to my house, jumping my friend, throwing sodas, ducking a fade. The treacheries had piled up. As I'm running towards them two bitches and three dudes get out of their vehicle. One of the guys has a bat. They're going to jump me. I was still running towards them knowing I'm about to get fucked up. Becky turns her car around and floors it trying to run over the guys with the baseball bat. She tells me get back in they're going to jump me. We pulled off. They hopped back in their car chasing us. We lost them for a second, got to a red light and suddenly two black Tahoe's pulled up on the sides. Within seconds at least six dudes and a couple of girls got out and are running at Becky's car. Zafree is screaming in the backseat like a bitch. Becky is mad as fuck calling them scary. Becky floors it and takes off

cause 3 vs 12 isn't a fair fight. I'm hanging out of the window cursing at them. One of the cars

is chasing us. They catch up close. We just hear loud "POP POP POP POP." They were shooting

at our car. Trying to shoot the windows. Luckily for us they had shit aim. Zafree is still

screaming like a bitch in the backseat. I'm hanging out of the window throwing all Becky's CD'S

at their car as they're shooting at us. I didn't give a fuck. Becky had a fishing weight in the car.

I chucked that heavy thing at their windshield. Becky is on the phone with 911. The lady is

telling me to get back inside the vehicle. Don't throw stuff at them and agitate them. The car

chasing us pulls off when they see Becky on the phone. We meet a police officer at the

nearest gas station. He takes a statement and names. Nothing ever happened to them. The

police department in that area is trash. They hardly ever do anything. After that incident

Becky and I were remarkably close. She knew I was a rider. I knew she was a rider. Grandma's

house was a hoarder's house. There was black mold growing everywhere. It had now been

festering for years. The walls were crumbling. The ceiling fell apart. The black mold was in the ventilation system. It had been spreading throughout the house for years. The second-floor

bathroom had a small leak behind the faucet that went untouched for years. The only

bathroom with a bathtub became so moldy the floor fell apart. There was no floor. There

were only support beams. Wide enough to fit your feet on them. If one of us were to fall. We

would have gotten severely hurt. The only other bathroom was located directly below the

second-floor bathroom. You could look down from the support beams and clearly see into the

other bathroom. It had the only working toilet. Grandma was suspicious. She would lurk

around the house eavesdropping. She could hear mom and dad coughing. Grandma started

spying on us in the bathroom. Just the grandkids. Probably because Mom and Dad were

capable of doing or saying something about it. Grandma would walk as quietly as she could on

the support beams in the second-floor bathroom. She would watch whoever was in the

bathroom below. She would listen to us use the bathroom. It was unnerving for all of us. We

would run the water or start the dryer to make noise. She thought the coughing came from

the bathroom or maybe she was just a pervert. I don't know why grandma did the things she did. Grandma didn't have insurance on the house. Not like she could afford it anyways. All her

bills were behind cause mom and dad mooched off her. She didn't want to get the mold

inspected because she knew the house would be condemned. The condition of the house was

THAT bad. The power in the house was shut off because grandma couldn't afford the bills.

Mom and dad were growing weed in the basement. When the weed was done Dean, Miles,

Melvan, and I had to cut and trim all their weed then place it in jars to cure it. I was expected

to sell the weed to my friends. I became their drug dealer. I didn't just sell their weed. I also

sold Dad's bipolar medication and mom's muscle relaxers. If I didn't sell enough for mom and

dad to buy the pain pills, they wanted and for us to have food, they would tell my brothers it

was my fault we weren't eating. I started selling to older people. One of my friends set me up

with this guy who was in a gang. I'm not going to mention the gang or names for my own

safety. I sold him weed and pills. He felt bad for me. He came from not shit parents too which

is why he joined a gang. He had me drop off packages. In exchange he'd buy whatever I had

and throw a little extra money my way for dropping off the packages. No questions asked. I knew the packages had heroin, coke, and guns. I did what I had to do to make sure I brought

home enough money to keep my parents off my back. To lessen the beatings. If I did a decent

job, they would treat me like a person. It didn't last for long and my connect ended up getting

hard time. The dude who took over was too sketchy. He was running a new operation that

included getting younger girls addicted to drugs and selling them out. I wasn't about to be set

up and prostituted. Mom and dad got kicked off their health insurance. No more pills. It got

bad. Eventually I sold all the weed and pills they had. They smoked what little they had left.

They were fiending so bad they smoked trim. Weed leaves and stems. Mom and Dad started

Miles, Dean and Melvin smoking weed. They were young. They said it was "time they all tried

it." I had just turned seventeen. Dean was fifteen, Miles was thirteen, Melvan was twelve. I

tried weed for the first time in a family smoke session. I liked it A lot, so did my brothers. We

started all craving weed. We accepted that our parents were going to spend all the money on

weed and pills. Smoking weed was an escape for us to distract ourselves from the neglect we

faced. That was the start of a weed addiction for all of us. We would smoke together every single day. Sometimes mom and dad wouldn't share their joints. It's because they would crush

their Oxy's, Norco's or perc's roll them up and smoke them. Sometimes they snorted them.

They didn't share with us not because they genuinely cared for our health but because they

were greedy addicts. That greed I'm grateful for. Weed addiction is something weed addicts

will deny. They'll say "it's not like other addictions" "I can quit anytime" but then get mad if

they haven't smoked in a day. Can't eat or sleep if they haven't smoked. I know because I lived

that life for many years. I smoked so much time and pain away. It numbed things. I'd be so

high I'd forget I was living in a basement sleeping on a concrete floor starving. I'd think to

myself "it's not that bad." I was so high it was easier to forget all my problems. The intrusive

thoughts would disappear the more I smoked. I smoked with my friends. The thing about

addiction is you can be addicted to anything. Addiction is something that will hold you back or

possibly ruin your life. I used to smoke an ounce to myself a week. 8-10 joints a day. Three

blunts. When I'd run out, I'd smoke roaches even though it would give me a massive

headache. I couldn't stand the feeling of not being high. I didn't like myself when the thoughts started flooding back in. Having clarity in my mind wreaked havoc. Reality isn't where I wanted

to be. I craved weed constantly. Rice was going crazy. Mom was responsible for watching him

while Grandma was at work. Grandma was in denial about how bad his condition was getting.

The doctors said it was dementia, but they didn't know the cause. Dementia itself isn't a

diagnosis. It's a serious of symptoms. Dementia always has a cause. Even with Rice losing his

memory Grandma refused to take his car keys though. The final straw for grandma was after

Rice got in his Subaru and drove off. Mom and grandma had to go to the police and report

him missing. I was happy. It pissed mom off. She said I was cruel. It didn't hurt my feelings

any. I didn't feel bad about his condition. After two days unfortunately they found Rice at a

gas station. Grandma took his keys after that. I remember them fighting for hours about it.

Rice was screaming "give me my keys woman" but after some time he would forget about

them. This same fight continued for a few weeks. Rice was no longer allowed to leave the

house. He was knit picking more things around the moldy house. He was aggressive with

Dean, Miles and Melvan who were now more than big enough to whoop his ass. Arguments

would get heated over the boys just trying to grab food out of the fridge because in his mind it was 4 years ago when we weren't allowed upstairs. With the entire house being so moldy

grandma didn't care where we were. We were allowed upstairs to keep constant supervision

on Rice. He would have bitch fits if we sat on the sofas. If we heard him coming out of his

room, we would all scramble to sit on the floor. If he weren't watching he'd wander outside.

He'd try to start his car without the keys. A few times he just started walking down the street.

Mom would get angry with me because when he'd wander, I wouldn't tell anyone. Eventually I

started dating this guy Abhorrent. He promised to save me. This chapter of my life wasn't

pleasant either.

Chapter 10

LIFE LESSONS

I started dating this boy named Abhorrent. He was just that. Things moved quickly in our

relationship. He was sweet and made me feel safe at first. I never felt so comfortable around a

boy before. He was a momma's boy, but he lived in his aunt's house. His mom was a junky

bitch who couldn't keep her life together. She also had a history of throwing her pussy at the

nearest man half her age who'd take it. Abhorrent's mommy issues became apparent quickly. I

was living in his room in the basement of his aunt's. She was an exceedingly kind and diligent

woman. I could tell from the judgement on her face though I was far from the only girl to be

staying over this much or maybe it was because he had other girls over. I worked a lot at a retirement community. I worked 12-14 hours a day. I made good money working as a

secretary, a care giver, helping the buildings manager and the assistant manager. I learned a

lot of things that helped guide me towards a good career path. I became a certified nursing

assistant. I helped take care of elderly people. I helped with rent roll. I helped call their

families. I listened to their problems. I would do their laundry. I changed adult diapers. I gave

showers. Changed bandages. Gave medications. Changed air tanks. It healed me a bit because

I was able to see that not all old people were like my grandparents. A lot of the people I met

were the sweetest. It was like I had one hundred grandparents that genuinely cared for me.

Abhorrent knew how much money I was making. He expected me to pay for everything. I paid

for our dates. I paid for his weed and mine. I paid a few of his bills on top of my own. My

parents were always holding their hands out. Expecting money. I gave it to them because

most of my stuff was still at my grandmas in the basement. They expected me to help

financially. Becky was my bestie. Her and Ab didn't get along. She didn't like him. He didn't like

her. Becky needed a job, so I vouched for her. This was the second time working with Becky. I had gotten her a job previously at chuck e cheese. She worked in the kitchen. It worked for a while until it didn't. I could tell Becky was jealous that I worked in the office with the managers. She was envious that she couldn't do what I did. She was envious I didn't have to wear a uniform. She attempted to transfer departments. The manager for my area asked me about her. I said they should give it to her because she was a hard worker. They checked her Facebook and seen it was full of drama and weed quotes. They couldn't have her at the front office because she wasn't good with people. She was always late and called in too often. I loved Becky but honestly, she was always getting me into trouble. She got into an argument online daily. Over the pettiest things. Whenever she had a disagreement with someone online, she dragged me into it. She used me as a bodyguard. Stepping away from our friendship years later allowed me to see that. Becky used me for a lot of things. She will never own up to it because it makes her sound like a horrible person. She used me when she got bored. When she wanted someone to make her feel pretty or special, she called me. When she wanted someone to vent to about her terrible boyfriend Tyler. Everything started going downhill.

Becky was jealous about the job position difference and jealous I was prioritizing time with Ab.

She didn't say what was bothering her. I could tell something was wrong when she started

making shady Facebook posts. At first, I assumed she was just beefing with someone. When

I'd asked who it was about, she would give a bogus ass answer. I knew it was about Ab. When

I asked her specifically, she finally said it. We argued and didn't talk for a week. We still

worked at the same place, so we saw each other a few times a week. Eventually we both

smoked and talked it out. We agreed we loved each other and cared enough about friendship

to work things through. Our friendship continued although it was obviously strained. Ab was

pissed. He started getting increasingly aggressive. He would call me all kinds of name and put

hands on me. Becky knew something was going on. Not only from how I was acting but

because she was going through the exact same thing. Her boyfriend Tyler wasn't good to her

either. He screamed at her, put hands on her then made her feel special by showering her in

gifts or compliments. Tyler didn't like me either because he said I was a bad influence on her. I

found that comical considering all the drama that was all Becky was in daily. In Tyler's eyes though he could control Becky. He couldn't control me. He knew I told Becky to leave his

funky ass. One day she invited me to go with her to her mom and stepdad's house to whom

she was close. She used to tell me all the time how much she loved her parents. How her

mom would do anything for her including "kill a bitch." We went over for her to visit her mom,

stepdad, and little siblings frequently. We smoked and talked with her parents. I noticed a pair

of shoes I had recently bought in the corner of Becky's mom's house. I bought a costume pair

of under armor shoes that was $250 to help me with my neuropathy in my feet. I thought I

lost them. Becky my "bestie" stole them and gave them to her mom as a birthday gift. I asked

Becky's mom right in front of her "where'd you get those shoes?." she said, "Becky gave them

to me for my birthday." I smacked my tongue on my teeth and just sucked a deep breath of

air in. She didn't bother trying to explain herself instead she went directly to Facebook saying I

was a fake friend and bringing up some dark things I didn't want to publicly speak about. Since

I was backed into a corner. I had no choice. I had a miscarriage with Ab directly after Becki

rear ended someone because she was driving high. We were on our way to work. Not even an hour after our accident I started bleeding. I bled through my pants. I bled all over the front

office chair. I was terrified, embarrassed, and shameful. I hadn't told my parents I was

pregnant. I was still living in grandma's basement. They would have kicked me out. I didn't

even know if I wanted to keep it. I was considering adoption. I wasn't far enough along to

decide. I told my manager I needed to leave immediately. Becky felt guilty so she offered to

take me to the emergency room. They took me back right away when they couldn't find the

heartbeat, they did an ultrasound. Months after this had happened Becky posted on Facebook

that I was lying even though she took me to the hospital. She claimed because I didn't let her

come back into the hospital room that I was lying. It was because she wanted me to be

publicly humiliated. She knew how deep of a sore spot that was. She knew that I was at risk of

being homeless. She felt embarrassed she'd gotten caught stealing shoes from her friend for

her mom. Instead of owning up to the fucked-up shit she did she needed to try and make me

sound like a horrible person so it would deflect what she'd done. It's ironic because she stayed

my friend after for months so if she really thought this why stay my friend? Why only post about it after you get caught stealing from your best friend? She couldn't say I was a bad

friend. She couldn't say I was fake. She couldn't say she had anything better than me. She

wanted people to dislike me as much as she disliked herself. She didn't leave the post up for

long after I posted medical records, ultrasound pictures and threatened to beat her ass. It

really hurt me though. I didn't want to publicly speak about it. I was embarrassed and hurt. It

was my fault. I got into that car knowing Becki was high and that she drives like shit. I felt

mostly guilty because I was happy, I had a miscarriage. I wasn't in a position to take care of a

child. I couldn't afford it. Ab and I would not have made good parents together. Our

relationship was extremely toxic. This is something I never wanted to speak about. This

happened when I was 17 years old. I never want to speak about it again. I deserve to have my

peace. Ab and I broke up. I was devastated and relieved at the same time. 4 months after

things ended with Ab a boy messaged me on Facebook. His name was William. I had hundreds

of unread dm's from boys, but I just felt like there was something more to Will. I gave it a

shot. He was kind, smart and a mechanic. The only bad thing was he was still living in his mom's house. Our first date was strange. We went out to eat in his fast car then went back to

his place to watch a movie. When we got there his mom was drunk fighting with his dad. His

mom starts yelling at the top of her lungs at him. Will's mom hops in his car and hits Wills

dad's car with Wills car. He rushes out. Leaves me completely alone in their house for 20

minutes. What a first date right? I'm sitting in Will's house who doesn't even know me by

myself for 20 minutes. Eventually Will came back and apologized. I asked him to take me

home. He was very apologetic. He said his mom's a little crazy but doesn't plan on living with

her long. He just graduated college. Will and I started dating after that. He ended up getting

kicked out of his mom's house. Will moved into his best friend Dylan's house right down the

street. Dylan lived with his mom, dad, and brother. They were the sweetest people I've ever

met. After visiting a few times and telling Dylan's mom what my living situation was like she

suggested I come live with them. Will and I lived in Dylan's house. We shared the spare room.

We lived there for 4 months then moved states together. Will was adopted. His biological

mom was an addict. His father was a drug dealer until he died. Will and his brother Ken were taken by child protective services and placed in the foster care system. Will and Ken suffered a

lot of abuse in the foster care system. He got adopted when he was five. He never really knew

his biological family. His grandma reached out and suggested we move in with her to get a

chance to know his biological family. We moved states away to live with his grandma. It was

an absolute nightmare. She was financially struggling and had no intentions of getting to know

her grandson. She just wanted someone to pay half of her bills. We lived in her house for all

of 3 months before we got our own place. I was working multiple jobs in an office, caregiving,

and event planning. I was working extremely hard and learning a lot about life. I enrolled and

started in school. Becky and I haven't talked for 2 years. One day a fake Facebook account

tagged me and her in a group chat. It was her from the fake account. The fake account sent a

bunch of pictures of us from happy memories we had. It said how we let men tear a good

friendship apart. It was so good I started crying. I loved her but I felt so betrayed by her. She

stabbed me in the back and didn't feel bad. We ended up talking. I genuinely hoped we could

be friends. I hoped we had both matured. She apologized. I apologized. We were in different chapters of our life. I thought to myself that the person I used to be so close with was still in there. When we first met it was because I told her Casey was messing with her boyfriend. She was sweet and genuine until the person she loved the most died. When her grandma died a piece of her did. I watched her become a different person after that. Selfish, mean, and airheaded. She felt like the world owed her something because she lost something. She didn't like ever being told she did something wrong because in her eyes she could never do anything wrong in a world where she lost her grandma. Sometimes she is truly incapable of self-reflection, but I know that's not true. If it were, she wouldn't be so angry when I tell the truth about her. She isn't angry because I'm lying, she's angry because telling my side of the story makes her look like a villain. We became friends again. Not long after she was expecting her first baby. I flew in from states away. I took time off work and school to visit her. We had so much fun catching up on life. She told me that she wasn't happy with Tyler. She wasn't physically attracted to him. She'd been having an affair with a guy. She said she liked the guy more than Tyler. Tyler eventually found out and flipped shit. Becky dumped the guy but stayed connected with him. I got my associate degree. I worked so hard to get there. Only Will and my new friends showed up at my graduation even though I invited my family and old friends. I didn't expect them to show up, but it still hurt. Nonetheless I was proud of myself.

Not long after Will lost his job. The apartment we were sharing became my responsibility. He burdened me financially. His mom suggested he come back to live with him. He left me all alone in the state by myself. I now had student loans, car payment, phone, rent, and insurance to pay all by myself. It was too much so I decided to move back too. Will and I broke up. I was pissed. I reached out to him because I loved him, but he pushed me away. I found out he was messing with other girls. I stopped reaching out. My parents finally had a house of their own. Mom and dad said they were sober and wanted me to move in so they could "make things right with me." I moved in. My room was a closet that was attached to Miles room. It was so small you couldn't even stand in it. A week after moving into my parents' house they informed me they expected me to pay half of the rent every month. I felt taken advantage of, but I paid for it. Dean was living in the basement which had two huge rooms and a private bathroom. He was working full-time yet he didn't pay a dime in rent. I was sleeping in a closet not even big enough to stand up in, but I had to pay half of the rent. Dean and I are 2 years apart in age. 3 weeks after I've moved in, they tell me they are $4,000

behind on rent. They hadn't paid rent for 7 months. Mom and Dad had no problem asking me

for money. I drained the last bit of my savings to pay the overdue rent so not only myself but

also my little brothers wouldn't be homeless. I was severely depressed at this point. I felt like I

had no one. Becky and I started hanging out more. It felt good. She was overwhelmed with

being a new mom. She told me all the time how unhappy Tyler made her. I told her all about

my adventures in the other state. We had so much fun together. I always offered to go to her

so she wouldn't have to make the baby go anywhere. I tried to make sure she knew it was

okay he was always with. I always made sure to reassure her. Will reached out to me. I

ignored him. He started emailing me and calling me from different numbers. I told him to go

fuck himself. I blamed him and told him he'd ruined my life. I quit my high paying job and

moved states for him then when things got hard because he couldn't hold a job he left to live

with his mommy. He only called me because he got kicked out again. I still loved him. I agreed

to meet up to talk with him. We talked for hours, cried, screamed at each other then ended up dating again. Dad, not even two weeks after I paid the overdue rent came up to my room

on the day, they knew I got paid and spoke.

"I need this month's rent."

"I just paid rent not even two weeks ago I have to pay my car and student loans."

"Then you can just get the fuck out of my house" he said through gritted teeth.

He was serious. He thought by threatening to kick me out. I would cave. Just give him the

money. I couldn't. If I didn't pay for my car, I wouldn't be able to get to work and I'd lose my

job. I said "okay." Mom and Dad were out of pills they bought from mom's "bestie." Mom and

Dad weren't sober. They've never been sober. It was all a lie to get me to pay for their habits.

Miles heard it all. He came into my closet of a room to console me. He agreed it was messed

up. I was kicked out after they knew I'd used all my savings to pay off their overdue rent. If I

hadn't, they'd be homeless. The landlord was in the eviction process. I should have used my

savings to move into a place of my own. I made a huge mistake. I was crying and trying to

pack my stuff. I wasn't prepared. I asked Miles if he could get me some garbage bags so I could just pack my stuff and go. He said of course. He goes downstairs to grab three trash bags. I can hear mom telling him "No fuck her these are our trash bags." That fucking bitch wouldn't have trash bags, let alone a house if I hadn't paid her overdue rent. I thought about going downstairs and punching her in the face. I decided I just wanted to leave peacefully.

This would be the last time I ever spoke to my parents. The last chance they EVER got. Miles yelled at mom "fucking move" and took the trash bags. I packed all my stuff up. Miles helped me move it into my car. I was bawling my eyes out the entire time. I couldn't believe I was so stupid. How could I ever trust my parents again? After everything they did to me. How could I be so stupid. I wanted so badly to believe that they were sober. Reality is even if they were sober, they would still be horrible people. I was such a fucking idiot. I left my mattress because I had no room for it. That night I was going to sleep in my car until I got a phone call.

Dean was calling me on Facebook over and over. He sounded frantic. He said I needed to come back to the house immediately. I thought there was an emergency like one of our parents overdosed or went to jail. I fly over to the house. When I get there the road is filled with cops. Melvin is in the back seat of one of the cop cars. He was violently banging his head against the window. I walked into the house immediately Dean told me I needed to take Miles. Mom starts flying from halfway across the room towards me. she's shaking. I'm on one side of the island. She runs up onto the other side of the island. She knew better than to run up on me. She's pointing her finger at me screaming "this is all your fault bitch." I yelled back "fuck you bitch I don't know what the fuck you're talking about I wasn't even here." Miles screams at mom "Shut the fuck up. fat bitch. It's your fault. You're always starting shit. Shut the fuck up. Shut up." Mile's shirt is covered in blood but it's not his. Mom screams "GET THE FUCK OUT OF MY HOUSE" over and over. Dean tells us "Guys need to leave our house" in a condescending tone. I told him, "Shut the fuck up freeloading basement dweller you don't pay rent but now you want to pretend to do something. Don't act like I was going to stay here dumb ass. I already left you called me back here." Dean turns red and stays silent. He knew better than to argue with me. Miles and I go to my car packed full of my stuff. Miles has a bag with some stuff but not much. I asked him what happened. Miles said after I left, mom was starting shit. She was mad he gave me trash bags, so she changed the Wi-Fi password. She said he didn't deserve Wi-Fi for helping me. Miles told mom that's stupid because we wouldn't they wouldn't have a house or Wi-Fi without me paying the overdue rent. Miles unplugged and took the entire Wi-Fi box to his room. Mom publicized up Melvin knowing he's got anger issues up to go take the Wi-Fi box from Miles. Melvan goes into Miles room talking crazy. Telling him "Give me the Wi-Fi box." Miles tells him "Fuck off and get out of my room." Melvan starts throwing Mile's stuff on the floor looking for the box. Miles shoves him and tells him again "get the fuck out of my room." Melvan says some delusional shit like "you're going to meet Jesus today." Miles started whooping his ass. Miles and Melvan had fought before. Melvan had gotten his ass whooped every time, but this time was the worst. The fight got so bad mom had to call the cops to break it up. When they broke it up Melvan in a fit of rage because he got his ass whooped started swinging and spitting on the cops so that's how he ended up in the back seat of a cop car. Melvan has always had anger issues. Everything now made sense. I thought the worst had come to pass. I rented a hotel room. The next day Miles didn't want to go to school, he wanted to take a day to reset. I told him it was fine, but he had

to go to school tomorrow. Skipping wasn't going to be a regular thing. He wanted a day to

reset. Two of his friends skipped with him and they spent time together. Around 5pm I got off

work. I picked up Miles and Will to tell him everything that happened while we went out to

get food. On the way to get food mom and dad pull up behind me in their bright red jeep and

they're following me. I started driving erratically because I was genuinely fearful of what their

plans were. I have Will call the police. They tell me to drive on a public road and meet them in

a motel parking lot. They tell Me and Miles to get out of the car. They tell Will to stay in the

car. Mom and Dad pull into the same parking lot. They're laughing. I will never forget this

moment. The officer tells me Mom filed an emergency restraining order on my brother's

behalf because he's seventeen. She says in the restraining order that I kidnapped Miles and

was planning to flee the state with him. If I have any contact with my brother by text, call or

email I will be immediately arrested. Miles says, "this Is fucking bullshit my mom kicked me

out." The cop said he doesn't care about the story. He must follow the judge's emergency restraining order. Miles says, "I DON'T give a fuck about the restraining order. I'm not going with them." The cop proceeds to tell Miles if he refuses, they're going to arrest him and hold him in the juvenile detention center. Miles says, "that's fine I'd rather be there than with those two crackheads." Miles leaves in a police car. I got in my car in tears. Shaking holding the restraining order. My mother is one of the vilest people to walk on this earth. She lied her ass off to humiliate me because I wouldn't give her drug money. I drove back to my hotel room. Mile's things are still there. I reach out to Paradise. I tell her what's happened. I told her how I was homeless. She didn't really care. She didn't want to get involved. I asked her if she could get miles his things back. I met up with her and gave her miles stuff. The next day I told Will goodbye, and I made an attempt on my life. Will called the police who intervened. They took me in handcuffs to the hospital and forcibly had me admitted. It was even more humiliating. I was placed in a wide padded room in a paper gown. GRIPPY SOCKS VACATION. Nurses came in every hour to ask me how I was feeling. Of course, I'm fine. To get released I had to explain my situation to a doctor. Once she heard what happened she put her hand on mine. She said something I've never forgotten "before the rainbow comes the storm. Things are, as you say

the worst now that means they can only get better, but you have to be here to see it get

better." She released me. I called Becky crying and she came and picked me up. She dropped

me off at my hotel room. I didn't talk to Will for a couple of days even though I knew he

meant well. I still felt betrayed. I felt if he cared so much why didn't he come to help. That

thought was unbelievably selfish and irrational. I know that now but then I didn't. I lived in a

hotel room for 5 months by myself. It was the loneliest point in my life. I had no idea if Miles

was safe. Paradise "Didn't want to get involved." It hurt a lot. Dean and Melvan were two

brainwashed brats who felt like I should have given all my money to mom and dad. They didn't

ever try to understand from my perspective. They only saw from their own because Dad

always told them that men were right. I'd always be wrong. I'd always be the bitch. Even

though I sacrificed my childhood trying to keep them alive. Trying to keep dad from beating

them. Trying to make sure they ate. I didn't do it for gratification. I did it because it was the

right thing to do. Which made it sting more when they didn't have my back. I felt alone. I felt like everybody had abandoned me. Becky and I weren't spending time together as much now that I wasn't financially stable. I couldn't pay for us to go out to eat or smoke her up like I usually did. I had to work a second job to afford to live in a hotel and pay my bills. One day I went to work, and I got called into the office by the manager. Mom called my job and told them she filed a restraining order against me on my minor brother's behalf. My job informed me that if a permanent restraining order were granted at the court date I would be let go. No reputable well-paying job would hire me, despite my credentials. This is exactly what my mom wanted. She wanted me to be out on the street with nothing. I was so angry I started crying. I told the managers I understood. I spent the next 2 weeks gathering hundreds of screenshots of Mom and I's conversations. I had evidence of Mom extorting me. Threatening me. Admitting to drug use. Admitting to me paying the overdue rent SO SHE wouldn't be evicted. Dean's Facebook call calling me back to the house. The court date hearing finally came. Will came with me and held my hand as we walked up the courthouse steps. My heart was beating so fast. I thought I was going to drop dead at any second. My entire career. Everything I'd worked so hard for was on the line. Mom's lies could ruin me. I would have nothing. I sit on

the bench outside my courtroom. Mom and dad walk in with Melvan and Dean. Dad gets up

and walks over to me sitting on the bench and says,

"You sure you want to do this little girl?"

Attempting to intimidate me. I said, "you didn't give me any choice."

He gritted his teeth. Sat back down with Mom but continued mean mugging me. I was

confused why Dean and Melvan were there. The officer opened the courtroom doors and told

mom, dean, and Melvan to enter first. Dad waited outside. I was told to walk in after them.

Will had to sit behind me. He was not allowed to stand at the stand with me. I had a file full of

hundreds of screenshots. The judge starts by saying what mom claims to have happened.

Michelle filed an emergency restraining order on Miles and Melvin's behalf. Michelle claims

that I kidnapped my 17-year-old 6-foot one football player brother Miles against his own

wishes. That I was a danger to both of my brothers. That I had threatened her with a weapon.

That I was a drug addict who partied all the time. That I was planning to flee the state with my

17-year-old brother. Michelle also claimed that I manipulated Melvan into fighting Miles. I was

"so dangerous." As the judge said all of this, my heart felt like it was going to explode out of

my chest. The judge let Michelle talk first. She said that she kicked me out of the house

because I was a danger to her sons. She said that she had evicted me. She said I had Miles for

an entire week and was planning to flee the state and take him with. I interrupted her.

"I have screenshots of Michelle admitting that I only had Miles for a day. I was not evicted. I

could have attempted to stay as I was a legal resident in the house, but I willingly left the

house after she and dad demanded rent a month early."

The judge raises his eyebrows and asks the officer in the courtroom to grab my screenshots.

Michelle starts saying that's not true. He cuts her off. He says He'd like to hear my side of the

story. I said.

"Your honor You'll have to excuse me for being nervous I have a lot to lose. My mom has

nothing to lose. My mom is a drug addict so is my dad— "

"Mom interrupts "LIAR!!!"

The judge slams his gavel.

"it's not your turn to talk."

I smiled and continued.

"They are taking me to court and using my brothers against me over money. They are broke because they spend all their money on drugs, they buy off the street. I willingly left the house after being financially drained. I paid all my parents overdue rent which was $4,000 worth and they kicked me out not even two weeks later my payday. My dad came into my closet which is where I lived a closet in their house and asked for rent a month early. Not because rent was due but because they needed money for their drugs. I was then kicked out of the home by Dad when I said no, I needed to pay my car payment and student loans. As I already said I was a legal resident and could have tried to stay but I knew how violent my parents are. It was best for my safety to leave. I left willingly and peacefully. My brother who is here today Dean called me not even an hour after I left and told me I needed to come back immediately. He did not tell me why over the phone. When I arrived at the house, I found out my brothers had a fight after I left the house. Mom and Dean both told me to take miles. Mom told miles to get out of her house. We left and not even a day later I was informed after my parents chased me in their car, they filed a restraining order against me on my brothers behaves. The fight I wasn't present for I was told by Miles who Michelle claims I kidnapped was over garbage bags-"

 The judge interrupted me. He looks at my mom.

 "Where is miles? Why isn't he here today?"

Mom says, "he would not come."

The judge just says, "You can't make your son come to court, but your daughter made him go with her? hmmm."

The judge looks back at me.

 "What happened with your brothers?"

"Your honor I was not present when the altercation occurred. When I had miles in my

custody, he told me Michelle instigated a fight between him and Melvan. She was mad he

gave me garbage bags to pack my stuff and peacefully leave the home. She changed the Wi-Fi

password, so miles took the Wi-Fi box to his room. Michelle encouraged Melvan who is here

in court today to get the Wi-Fi box out of Mile's room. This is how the altercation allegedly

occurred but again I can't for sure say as I was not present in the home. I only know what I

was told."

The judge looks disgusted at Michelle and says-

"You say it's your daughters fault they fought but is it true she was not present at the time of

the altercation?"

Michelle starts jumbling her words "it- it was her fault."

Judge says He's ready to hear the witness's statements. I thought to myself, witnesses? Then I

realized. My brothers were about to testify against me. I was choking back tears. I felt so betrayed. Dean was the first to be sworn in, probably because he was eighteen. The judge

sighs deeply and asks him "What happened?"

Dean immediately says "She's a bad person. She does drugs and parties all the time."

The judge interrupts dean and says, "Have you witnessed this personally?"

Dean shakes his head. The judge sucks in a deep breath. It was obvious he was losing

patience. He asks, "Did you call your sister back to the house to pick up Miles?"

"Yes, but she's out partying and- ".

Judge cuts him off "let me stop you there, so you're saying that you called your sister to pick

up your brother up after an altercation but now you're saying that she's such a bad person and

a drug addict she shouldn't have had him. Why did you call her then?"

Deans entire face turns red. He looks frustrated at mom. Judge says,

"Why are you looking at her? let me ask you a question son, did your mom tell you to say any

of this?"

Dean immediately nods his head and says, "yes but-."

Mom yells from the stand "No I didn't."

The judge asks, "Do you know what perjury is?"

"What?"

Judge sighs deeply. "Get off my stand." Dean waddles away in shame and sits on the benches.

Melvan is sworn in. Judge asks,

"Was your sister present at the time of the altercation?"

Melvan says, "no but we wouldn't have fought if she had just done what mom said."

The judge asks, "how long was your brother with your sister before your mom filed the

restraining order?"

Melvan- "I don't know a day or two."

The judge says, "Did your mom tell you what to say?"

"Yes."

"Okay, you can get down from the stand."

Michelle interjects. Trying to argue with the judge. He slams his gavel down.

"I've heard enough from you, I'm ready to make my ruling."

My heart was thumping out of my chest. The judge tells everyone to stand. He looks directly at Michelle and says "I think you should be ashamed that you have acted this way. That you treated your own daughter this way. That you have wasted everyone's time." Mom interrupts the judge again.

"She is dangerous- ".

Judge slams his gavel "one more word and I will hold you in contempt."

"This young woman is no threat to your family. It is obvious you have wasted my time. You should be ashamed your family is this broken. I find in favor of the defendant the restraining orders are hereby dissolved." I started crying. A huge weight lifted off my chest. Mom was fuming. She tried to storm out.

The judge said, "you will wait here and let her leave first."

Will and I scurried out of the court room. I damn near ran to the car. I was so happy. I was

bawling my eyes out. Tears of relief. So many emotions but freedom felt so sweet. I didn't feel

chained down anymore. I wasn't walking on thin ice of going to jail or losing my job. I could

call my brother again. I could see him again. I felt so relieved. I was still suffering the

consequences of trusting my parents. I was still homeless. I kept applying to apartments and

getting denied. I was really confused. I tried to login to credit karma. My account was locked. I

requested to get in Via email. My account was locked due to suspicious activity. I found out

mom stole my social security number. She used it to take a $3,000 loan out in my name. She

never paid for it. Obviously. It damaged my credit so much I was getting denied by every

housing option I applied to. I wrote letters to the credit bureau telling them I did not take this

loan out. It was identity fraud. It took 3 months to get it removed off my credit. I was

homeless for a total of 5 months. I couldn't always afford to sleep in the hotel room.

Sometimes I had to sleep in my car. On those days I'd take a bird bath at the gas stations near my jobs. It was rough. Being alone. Being hungry. Never being sure of tomorrow. Not having

clean clothes. When I did eat it was very unhealthy. Whatever I could afford. Mostly cups of

ramen, ravioli, Tv dinners. I began gaining weight rapidly due to the unhealthy and

inconsistent eating. My body was in starvation mode retaining fat. Not even 1 month after the

court date Paradise texted me. It wasn't to check in on me. It was to ask me on mom and

dads' behalf for money because they were being evicted out of the very house, they kicked me

out of. Yeah. Ironic, isn't it? I said hell no. Fuck them.

Becky was beefing with random girls on Facebook. She invited me into the group chat. I of

course started arguing with the girls defending my friend. My mentality was If my friend has

beef with you so do I. Not even 20 mins after I'm legit about to meet up and fight one of them

for her (which I know fucked up priorities I was homeless like humble myself). Becky texts me

and tells me to chill, they're all cool now. She used me like a bodyguard. Got me involved to

defend her for nothing. They ended up inviting Becky and me to a roast group Facebook page.

It had a thousand people. The point of a roast group page is exactly that. It's a shallow page

for people to just diss looks and put people down about anything. I don't know why Becky

wanted to be on that page, just because she enjoyed drama. I started slugging people after I had left a comment and someone's daughter who was nineteen said something smart and the mom was one of the page admins. She said no talking about people's kids and started going in on me. I said how the fuck are you going to say no kids but she's nineteen, in the group and came for me first? The math wasn't mathing. We got into it heavily. This was one of the original girls I was arguing with on Becky's behalf. I ended up becoming a target on the page. I got posted, so I posted back. I ended up becoming one of the top roasters on the page. The only thing people could slime me about was me being overweight which bothered me, but I could always think of something worse. I came from two vile ass parents who spent every day of my childhood verbally degrading me. I'm exceptionally good with hurtful words. Becky was annoyed and envious of all the attention surrounding me. I don't know why because it wasn't good. I eventually wanted out of the group, and I left. Becky started acting funny. Hanging out with me less. One day she told me her baby was sick and she couldn't hangout. That was a lie. She was at a pool party with the people I had gotten into it with on the roast group page.

When I confronted Becky about it, she said I was controlling and a bad friend. It escalated.

Becky started making Facebook posts how "I'm a snake and I wanted to be her" and posting

once again about my personal life. I was invited back to the roast group page and tagged in a

bunch of posts of people making fun of me being homeless. Becky told everyone not only that

I was homeless but also about being sexually assaulted, and my miscarriage. It was one of the

evilest things I experienced in my life. Not long after I found out I was 4 weeks pregnant. I had

hundreds of people making fun of my situation. Telling me I should kill myself. Telling me I'm

worthless. Telling me I'm lying about my pregnancy. Telling me my baby will be ugly or

deformed. Telling me they hoped my baby died. I wouldn't wish that on my worst enemy. I

fought back. I found out tea about everyone talking shit and I exposed them all. I didn't back

down. I didn't let them know how much it hurt me. I had sunk down to their level of vile

cruelty. I let my character change. I showed them the evil bitch they wanted to see. I exposed

Becky for not only being a liar, a cheater, and a fake bitch in general. I posted eleven

screenshots a week before her birthday of her talking shit about all her closest friends. None

of them showed up for her birthday. I could have posted much worse, and I chose not to. I

could have posted the screenshots of her telling me how much she hated her baby daddy

Tyler on whom she is completely financially dependent. Where she said she only stays with

him because she needs him but isn't attracted to him. I could have posted the screenshots of

her calling and texting me after she got drunk with her toddler in the car crashed it and then

asked me to get them. I could have posted the video she sent me of her 2-year-old sucking on

a weed pen and her laughing about it. I could have posted so much more than I did. I could

have kept these things secret. I'm done keeping a bitch's secrets who didn't keep mine. Becky

begged me to stop posting. She wanted to be friends again. She said she only did all of that

because she was hurt. She told me how much she loved me and how she'd never been as

close to another girl as she was with me. At one point I felt that way too. I was going through

pregnancy emotions. I missed my friend despite everything she'd done and everything I'd done

in retaliation. We became cool again and I deleted my Facebook. Things felt weird. She was

constantly comparing herself to me. Whenever I said I had a rough day, hers was always

worse. Whenever I had something good happen like a job promotion or raise and I was just

excited sharing my day with my friend she would change the subject. I saw the envy. I ignored

it. Becky was always complaining about Tyler. Always complaining about how hard it was being a mom and how I wasn't ready. Tyler and her often yelled at and hit their toddler. He

started having worse and worse tantrums. Becky couldn't really take him anywhere because

he'd have a meltdown and throw himself to the ground screaming and crying. He was

aggressive towards other children. I saw the kind of Mother Becky was and I made excuses.

She's only tired. She's just overworked. It's simply hard being a mom. Will and I had moved

into an apartment and then gotten a house. We had gotten engaged and married in a

courthouse. I didn't want a big wedding. I didn't have a dad to walk me down the aisle. I didn't

talk to my siblings at that point. I had cut ties with everyone in my family. Until one day

Paradise called me. Miles was in the hospital. His appendix had ruptured. He had to have

emergency surgery to have it removed. He was okay but he wanted me to visit him. I was 6

months pregnant at the time. I had not publicly announced my pregnancy due to not wanting

my family to know. Paradise, however, had already told mom and dad. When I got to the

hospital, I was expecting to meet paradise in the parking lot. Mom got out of paradise's car.

She was crying and shaking. She hugged me. I froze. She said she was "so sorry" "it was all dad's idea." I knew she was lying. I just froze. I said it was okay and brushed her off me. It was weird. Mom then said, "omg you're carrying my first grandbaby I can't wait to be a grandma." I held in internal laughter. A grandma? Please bitch you have to be a mother first. Paradise, Mom, and I headed up to miles room. He was fine. He was talking about football. He's always been the strongest of the boys. Took it like a champion and recovered quickly. He was excited about being an uncle. I saw Melvan and dad walk in. Melvan came and hugged me said he missed me. Dad gritted his teeth and ignored me. Fuck you too you. Balding bitch. I thought to myself. Eventually after 20 minutes dad said Hi to me after everyone left the room. He asked if I knew if it was a girl or a boy. I told him it was a boy. He asks if Will and I were still together, I told him we were married. We married in a courthouse since I didn't have any family. He was silent after that. He said he was sorry for how things went. It seemed genuine. I thought about telling him how mom blamed him but decided best to keep it to myself. I knew dad didn't file a restraining order because of one. He hates cops and judges and two. He's a 3-time felon, he hates court rooms after being in them so many times. After that I was allowed to visit Miles and Melvan at the house. Dean ignored me. He ignored everyone in the house. He had started dating a religious nutjob her name was Gollum. That's not really her name but to me it was. I knew her family from when I lived in the small country town with my sister. Gollum was a racist right wing religious whack job. She was really a crazy one. She said watching football was a sin because it was gambling. She said that rock and roll music was a sin because it was the devil's music. She made Dean her little bitch. She said Black people belonged in service working jobs. She said Black people and white people together is a sin. She said all Black people were ghetto. Dean lost his entire personality but honestly, he never really had much of one. Dean's always been like a sponge. He absorbed and became whatever was around him. He went through so many phases. "Trying to find himself." Him "finding the lord" was his worst phase. He was a pompous conceited douchebag. He still didn't pay rent at 19 living in mom and dad's basement. Gollum was over nearly every day. She would walk into their house and say nothing to no one. She believed she was better than everyone. With a face and mindset like that it's a mind puzzler for sure. Dean looked at all his family with disgust. Eventually Mom and dad found out the landlord filed an eviction notice against them

again. They asked me for money. Without hesitation I said no. I had money too. I just didn't

care to make other people's problems my own. No one helped me when I was drowning so

fuck em.' They began packing their things. Bum ass Dean moved in with Gollum's religious

nutjob family because he wasn't invited to move into the next apartment with mom and dad.

The last few weeks before they got evicted mom started sleeping in the basement on the floor

with the mattress I had left behind. She started sneaking out. She was cheating on Dad with

her ex-boyfriend. It's ironic it was bologna. (Bologna's story is on page 5). Dad found out

flipped shit. Started drinking again. He was mostly verbally violent probably because he knew

Melvan and Miles were more than big enough to whoop his ass. He would destroy things in

the house. Mom one day while dad was at work said that she wanted paradise to meet

Bologna. Paradise begged me to come with her because she didn't want to go alone. I

reluctantly agreed. Paradise says she's going to drive us so if it's weird we can leave. Bologna

didn't have his own car. His friend drove him from Louisiana all the way up to Illinois. They

rented a hotel room. Bologna and his friend shared a hotel room together. Paradise and I are expecting to go out to a nice restaurant to eat, right? no Bologna and his friend are cooking in

a crockpot in the hotel room. Things just kept getting worse. Bologna is already wasted. Mom

starts drinking glass after glass of wine. Paradise and I are sitting in the hotel room chairs

while mom and bologna make out with tongue right in front of us. One of the top ten most

disturbing things to witness is your mom being a hoe. Mom spent so many years knit picking

Paradise and I about how we dressed and yet here she was cheating on a 20-year marriage.

Bologna and his friend want to step outside to smoke so paradise and I have to come. We got

outside and as they were smoking weed, he and his friend started telling a story. Bologna's

friend says they caught a felony after they got hyped up on crack and robbed a gas station at

gunpoint. They thought it was the funniest story they'd ever told. Mom could tell from

Paradise and my face we were horrified. Did this dude really think telling us her daughters this

story would make us like him? Did he really find crack and robbery that fucking funny?

Disturbing. Mom grabs bologna's arm and says, "look at how big his arms are." I text paradise

even though I'm right next to her "can please leave?" She tells mom we're probably going to

leave soon. Bologna and his friend say "the foods almost done you've got to try it. It's jambalaya." At this point it's already been 2 hours and the food in the crock pot isn't ready.

Paradise, feeling pressured agrees to wait. We waited an additional 45 minutes, and the food was finally ready. I only ate plain white rice because I'm a vegetarian. My morning sickness was awful, the smell of the food I ran to the bathroom and puked. This was my chance. I kept puke to go baggies in my purse. I told paradise we had to go cause my morning sickness was so bad. which it was but also, I just wanted to go home. Dean told dad about mom's sleep over with her ex-boyfriend. Not sure what happened at home after that, but it wasn't even 2 weeks later. Mom abandoned Miles and Melvan with Dad and ran off with Bologna to Louisiana. While all of this was going on I was 42 weeks pregnant and set to be induced. After 10 hours of labor my heart rate and my sons were so high, we were at risk of dying. Since I was already marked a high-risk pregnancy, physically exhausted, and had a history of heart problem I was rushed in for an emergency C- section. Paradise and Will were not allowed to come in with me. It was the start of the pandemic. Not much was known about covid but there were a lot of restrictions. I was taken in by myself with the doctor and two male nurses.

The doctor administered pain medication. She began making the incision. I screamed out in pain. I could feel everything. I felt like I was being sliced in half. It was one of the most painful things I'd ever fucking felt in my whole life. Doc says, "oh you can feel that." No shit, I thought to myself. She gives me more pain medication. Immediately continuing the incision. I scream even louder because it fucking hurts. She gives me more pain medication. At this point its kicking in. I'm so high. I'm going in and out of consciousness. I started vomiting on myself. I'm choking on my own puke. I'm too weak to move. The two male nurses who are supposed to be helping me are watching the doctor make the incision. My heart rate and blood pressure start elevating causing the machine to make a beep. The two nurses yell "she's choking suction." The last thing I remember is the tube going in my throat to suck out the vomit. I nodded out. Nothing but Blackness. I came back for a second and heard my son cry and then blackness again. Peaceful pitch-black nothingness. When I woke up, I had a baby and excruciating pain. I kept vomiting as a side effect from the pain medication they had given me earlier. Every time I puked it pulled my c section stitches it busted open twice. They had to redo the stitches. I refused any more pain medication. I didn't want to become dependent on it. I was fearful of at some point liking it too much and becoming an addict like my parents. I accepted ibuprofen and Tylenol. I was allowed to leave the hospital 2 days later. Recovery was awful. I couldn't stand up straight. I had a lot of pain. I could barely move. I was bed ridden but taking care of a newborn. Will's job didn't allow him to have time off. He was forced to go back to work even though I could barely walk. I struggled deeply but I made sure my beautiful baby boy got what he needed. Dad delt with the eviction himself. He moved into an apartment just big enough for him, Miles, and Melvan to have their own rooms. He was emotional. Pearl was never an independent person. He always needed someone to take care of him. Someone to be his emotional and physical punching bag. He started communicating online with an ex-girlfriend of his from 22 years ago. 3 weeks after mom ran out, he texted me saying "Take care of your brothers". Pearl ran off with an ex-girlfriend in Louisiana. The apartment's rent had not been paid since Pearl moved them in. They were being evicted. Pearl left Miles and Melvan at 16 and 17 years old in an apartment they were being evicted out of.

Still in high school. Miles was able to continue and get his high school diploma. Melvan

dropped out. I attempted to take in both of my brothers. I had a newborn. I didn't trust

Melvan. He had a history of theft and Violence. I knew at all costs I would pick my son over

anyone. I did a trial run to see if things would be okay for Melvan and Miles to stay. I had

them over at my house for a few days. On the second day $200 and a gaming controller was

stolen. I knew Melvan stole it. He always stole shit. I blamed both Melvan and Miles. I felt like

Miles knew he stole it and was covering for him cause bro code. He had no idea. I found out

much later. I lashed out at both. I told them they couldn't stay. Miles didn't talk to me for

weeks. He eventually reached out and said he didn't know Melvan stole it. Miles and I

reconciled. He lived with me for a bit before moving out and living with his friend and then his

girlfriend. Becky convinced me to join TikTok. She said it was a fun app to express yourself.

Kept going on and on about how she was going to be famous from it. It's funny how things in

life play out. My first TikTok videos were moronic. Shallow cringey Thirst traps. At some point

I decided I wanted to begin pursuing something I wanted to do. I had a passion for art. I always wanted to be a makeup artist, a painter, or a drawer. I wanted to hone my skills. I

began making makeup transitions. I started to gain traction on TikTok. Becky started making

the exact kinds of videos I did. It was creepy. She claimed it was because it was "Just the

trend." It was obvious she was envious of the traction I was getting. She was upset I wouldn't

make videos with her. I wouldn't tag her. I didn't want anyone who posted their location on

my TikTok. I didn't trust her. I found out a month after having my son. There were multiple

girls involved. He didn't meet up with them. He chatted and sexted online with them. It made

me so angry. I made my first extremely viral TikTok. I took the PlayStation 4 I gave to Will that

had a faulty HDMI port and I smashed it with a hammer. I attempted to light it on fire. I

posted It publicly. I sent it to will and told him to gather his shit off the lawn when he came

home. He slept outside the first day. Willingly. Then stayed at his mom's. Then at a hotel. The

video of me smashing the ps4 and trying to light it on fire had over ten million views. I

officially had 50,000 followers. Women from all over praising. Men sending me death threats.

This was the second time I realized the power of the internet. I realized any comment or video could be "The one." I was riding the wave. Will suggested he get a tattoo to prove his

dedication and that I film it. I filmed us going to the tattoo shop. Will got a huge tattoo in bold

letters on his arm that says, "I cheated on everybody." Will has never been faithful in any

relationship he ever had. He had cheated on every single woman he dated. This video also

went viral. Amassing over seven million views. I ended up doing an explanation video about

destroying the PlayStation 4. Explaining it wasn't in good shape. I only destroyed it because

Will didn't remember his login information. He lost all his game progress and purchases. He

was never able to recover it. Becky started acting weird towards me. She started posting

cryptic things. She was jealous. These cryptic posts would be things like "I don't even be liking

my friend I just be kicking it with them because I'm bored." I asked her who it was about. She

said, "general post." Bullshit bitch. Say what you mean. Say it with your chest. I stopped

posting about drama. I posted my first makeup Storytime. I was gaining and gaining followers.

The more followers I amassed the more Becky treated me like shit. Often copying my videos

using the same sounds I'd pick that weren't even trending. My followers began attacking her for copying my videos. I made several videos defending her even though I agreed it was creepy. It wasn't long after this I began getting hate comments with my personal information like my son's name and my home address on my videos. Someone was pretending to be my stalker. THINKING it would scare me off TikTok. I didn't know for sure, but I was suspicious that it was Becky. Will and I agreed to go to marriage counseling. After a few months, He moved back in. Our relationship was better, but I didn't trust him. I was bitter towards him. I couldn't forgive easily. The election was starting. As an open pansexual woman, I of course wanted to see Donald trump lose. I think he's a racist homophobic selfish rich prick. I don't think Biden is amazing, but he was better than trump. I made it public that I was voting for Biden. I made it public that Donald trump has been exposed multiple times for being a pedophile. Openly admitting to watching underage pageant girls get dressed. Saying he would sleep with his own underaged daughter. Several disgusting racist and homophobic comments. I posted about these things because I didn't want people that liked trump following me. I didn't want to build a following on people who I knew wouldn't support me for who I am. I had no idea that Becky was right wing. Hell, I don't think she even knew. She'd NEVER cared

about politics before that year. She only became right wing because Tyler was. Tyler who is

mixed and racist along with his WHITE mother were right wing nutjobs. Tyler referred to other

Black people as monkeys. He said the N word hard R. I will never forget when Tyler found out

he wasn't Puerto Rican and was black he said he wasn't an N word. Becky laughed. I felt very

uncomfortable. I'm just as wrong for staying friends with a racist. I knew how Becky was and I

stayed her friend. Guilt by association. Becky also said the N word without hesitation. We

fought about it several times. She said if her Black friends didn't have a problem with it "it

didn't matter." "If its in a song then white people can say it." She even said she was Italian so

she can say it. Which she isn't even Italian. She just has a huge fucking nose. She said I was on

a moral high horse. Shit I was. I promise you though I don't give a fuck. When I went to the

schools on the west side. I saw how my nonwhite friends were treated by white teachers,

white business owners and white police officers. I heard them talk and listened closely. I've

been lucky enough to hear their experiences. I will never KNOW their struggles but being aware of them helps the world. Educating yourself is a good thing. I'd rather be on a moral high horse than an ignorant bitch. Becky made post after post responding to my generalized posts, I made about Donald trump. Saying anyone who voted for Biden was a "Sheep" and "loved pedophiles" because he "Sniffed kids." I blocked Becky. I was so tired of her shit. She would NEVER say when she had an issue. Passive aggressive bitch. The delusional bitch also got all her facts off Facebook. She tried to argue about covid being fake when I worked in a hospital and a retirement home. I knew what was going on. I saw it every day. I saw people getting sick. I saw people die. I helped sick people. Becky was cheating on Tyler again. She had started an affair with a scraggly alcoholic coworker who was 5 years older than her. His name is Creep. Creep knew Becky was living in Tyler's mom's house. He didn't care because he was living in his ex's house. Still fucking her. I'm sure still lying to her also. Creep drank every single day. He had blonde hair and bright blue eyes that looked like flashlights. One day Becky calls me and tells me that she's fighting with Tyler because he went through her phone and found out about her cheating on him again with another man. She said their relationship was horrid.

She wasn't attracted to him and never had been. The only reason she ever liked him was because he financially provided for her. He cleaned. He took ok care of their son. Sure, he yelled and hit him but in Becky's eyes a father is a father. Probably because her father was dead. She didn't know what a dad was supposed to look like. Her dad lured gay men to rob them but one day he killed one. He got put to death. It's sad but you can't let your parent's criminal past justify you being a shit parent. You can't repeat the cycles. You're supposed to break them. Becky and Tyler fought consistently before Creep entered the picture, but it was worse. I had seen Tyler pull Becky down by her hair. Shove her. Call her a bitch and a whore.

Slapped their 2-year-old so hard he fell on his face. Drag their 2-year-old by his arms. Tyler would drive at crazy speeds swerving around with us in the vehicle when he was mad at Becky. I can only imagine what went on behind closed doors. One day Becky called me and asked if I could hangout. She said she was having an awful day. She said Tyler raped her. She wanted me to come over. Tell Tyler's mom we were going bowling. I assumed this meant we were going bowling. I dropped everything I was doing. I told Will what was going on and that I would be out late. I told Will I could convince Becky to stay with us and bring her son. When I got to Becky's we went inside and talked with Tyler's mom for a bit. Becky seemed normal. We

left to go "Bowling." I hugged her and asked her if she was okay, was everything okay? All she

said was "I think he raped me; I don't know but if anyone asks, we were together all night." I

was very confused by all of this. She proceeds to explain we are going to a bar in Wisconsin to

meet up with her side piece from work Creep. I was like ok... this is fucking weird. She drives

us to this bar in Wisconsin to meet up with Creep. I'd never met him before, only heard stories

from her. Becky goes to the bathroom and leaves creep and I alone at the bar. I tell creep you

know I really care for my friend are you serious about her? I know you're living in your ex's

house, are you over it? Creep looks me in my eyes clearly already intoxicated and flat out says

"I'm still in love with her but like it's over." Now ladies, you know damn well from

experience... we all have that one toxic ex. Living together? Still in love? But it's over... Yeah

right. RED flag after red flag. Becky comes back and she can tell I already don't like Creep. I

gave her THAT look. The look where you tell your bestie with your eyes bitch what the fuck.

Becky starts knocking down shots and iced teas. I had one bloody Mary that I didn't finish.

Truthfully, I don't like alcohol. I was watching Becky throw down shot after shot. I'm thinking

to myself is this bitch for real. She drove us. She's so drunk she can barely get up from the bar.

It's now 2am. We've been at the bar for about 4 hours. She says let's go. I said ain't no way

you're driving me. I have to make it home. I'll drive us. I was annoyed. Creep starts laughing

and says that he doesn't drive after he drinks that Becky ALWAYS drives him. He leaves his car

at the bar. I asked, "so you guys do this all the time?" Creep says yeah this is our regular spot.

Becky had drunk and drove before, but she was doing this regularly? She already had SRT

insurance which is special driving insurance for all the accidents she had while driving high, yet

now she was driving regularly drunk. This annoyed me. I was disgusted by how my "friend"

was composing herself. I started driving HER car back from Wisconsin to Illinois which was

about a 30-minute drive. Becky sits in the backseat with Creep. They're making out and

moaning loudly. Creep fingered Becky in the backseat while I drove her car back into town.

You just got raped but who am I to judge how you manage things. Reflecting now on the

situation she made that up knowing my history with sexual assault she used me as an excuse

to lie to meet up with Creep. Why lie right? Well let's break it down. Becky was living in Tyler's mom's house. At any moment Tyler's mom could put her out and keep their son under the basis that Becky didn't have stable living conditions. She had both alcohol and weed dependency. She knew that so she used me. When we got into town, I decided fuck this. I'm not wasting anymore of my day on her. I didn't want to go out in the first place. I drove straight to my house. I told her to let me know when she made it home. Slammed her car door. Rushed inside my house thankful I made it. I told Will everything. He was pissed. He didn't want me to hangout with Becky anymore. He said not only was she a bad influence, but she was dangerous and mentally unstable. He wasn't wrong. If I had gotten drunk Becky would have been driving and could have very well killed someone else or us. Becky took off that night drunk her in car with Creep. Tyler called me not even 20 minutes after I got home. I put him on speaker phone so Will could listen. Tyler is crying. I can hear his and Becky's 2-year-old son crying saying "Where is mommy". Tyler proceeds to tell me that Becky has been out for an entire month staying out late every night and coming home drunk. She's been neglecting her son. He says he knows she's cheating on him again. He doesn't know what to do. He said I was the only friend he trusted. He asked if I could talk to Becky. Becky to this day I'm sure has no

idea Tyler called me and talked shit about her for an entire hour. I never told her. Maybe that

makes me a fake friend? I don't know. It's not like she was a good friend either. I agreed with

Tyler. She was fucking up. She was being a shit mother. She was calling off her job regularly

because she was hungover. She ended up getting fired. I distanced myself from Becky. After

this incident I started taking longer replying to texts because I was still annoyed. I felt drained

dealing with her. It didn't feel like a friendship. It felt like a trap I couldn't escape. The hate

comments from fake accounts amplified during this period. I'd delete the comment and block

the account. Within an hour a new user4857358 left the exact same comment. Originally, I

thought it may have been Tyler making the fakes. Becky told me she was mad at me because

Tyler told her I was making posts calling her dumb. I didn't. I said anyone voting for Donald

trump is dumb. I went to block Tyler and already had Tyler blocked so either Becky was lying,

or he created a new account. I couldn't tell but I sat in silence with my suspicions. It was

Becky's birthday. We weren't doing good friendship wise. I felt guilty for ruining her birthday the year before. I had planned a hotel trip. We were going to chill smoke and do a little acid.

She had never done acid before and wanted to try it. It was one room with two beds and one

room with a kitchen/living room area. I told Becky I was going to bring Will and my son

because I wanted someone sober to be there and didn't want to be apart from my son for

long. Becky said she wanted Creep to come. I knew it was going to go terribly but it was her

birthday. When we all got to the hotel Will and Creep went inside to handle the room. The

room reservation when I Booked online was only half which is ridiculous because it was $100

and then an additional $100 upon arriving. I had Chase bank. My card was lost so I had

cancelled it. I didn't have a card that day. I had no idea that the room was going to charge an

additional $100 upon arriving because I didn't read the reservation. That was entirely my

stupidity and fault. I should have read and observed things more carefully. Will was searching

through his wallet to find his card when Creep offered to pay for half of the room as part of a

gift to Becky since he had gotten her nothing for her birthday. Creep was already shit faced.

He had brought fifty jello shots, yeah fifty. Two bottles of Vodka and a bottle of tequila. All the

bottles had already been mostly consumed...by him. Becky keeps saying she wants Creep to leave. She wants Tyler and her son to come. She says she wishes she would have listened to

me and just invited Tyler and her son. I reminded her...It's her birthday. She can do what she

wants. At this time, I had no idea Creep had paid for half of the room. Will had not told me

yet. Becky and I had both consumed a tab. If you've never done acid, you don't know that it

amplifies all your feelings. Not even 20 minutes into our trip, she wants to step out again. We

are laughing and joking around having a wonderful time. She said she doesn't like Creep lately.

He's a bum. He's an alcoholic. He didn't even get her anything for her birthday. He isn't good

to her like Tyler is. I told her to call Tyler. She did. We go back up to the room. Becky tells

creep that Tyler and her son are on the way. Creep starts angry crying and downing jello

shots. He asked Becky and I at least twenty times if we wanted a jello shot. Over and over. We

kept saying no and getting annoyed by the constant pressure of being asked. We locked

ourselves in the bathroom. We sat on the floor joking about life. Then she said that Creep's

alcohol problem had been bleeding over to her life. I told her he wasn't good enough for her.

Becky pulled out her phone and recorded a TikTok. I told her you better not post that. She said of course not its just for memories and I only used TikTok for the filter. We stayed in the

bathroom reminiscing on the floor for the next 30 minutes. It felt like five to us. Tyler knocked

on the hotel door. Tyler and Will went to the other room and started talking. Creep was

sloppy drunk. He was standing trying to talk to Becky and he almost passed out while

standing. He caught himself at the last second. Barely saving himself from slamming his head

against the corner of a hanging hotel flatscreen. I went to the next room. There was so much

tension. Creep in front of Tyler was groping Becky's ass. Multiple times she shoved Creep off

her. Creep not getting any attention from Becky with a glass full of pure tequila goes to the

bed Becky's son is on. Tyler and will and Becky are in the other room. I'm watching my son like

a hawk and Becky's because I don't trust creep. Creep is touching all over Becky's son's leg.

falling over on him. He spills a bunch of tequila on Becky's 2-year-old son. I called him over

onto my bed and I asked if he wanted to play to lure him away from creep. Creep gets up and

sits on my bed with his now half empty cup of tequila. I told him please stay over there cause

he's spilling alcohol everywhere. He ignored me. Stays on my bed. Steady touching the 2-year-old trying to hold a conversation with him. This guy is fucking weird. I flat out tell creep

"You're embarrassing yourself. You need to stay over there. Why are you trying to talk to a 2-

year-old talk to your girl". Creep gets up mumbling some bullshit under his breath and walks

into the bathroom which is connected to the bedroom. He's so drunk he can barely walk. The

door is WIDE OPEN. He almost falls over, so he grabs the toilet paper holder for stability

ripping it out of the wall then proceeds to piss with the door wide open for all of us to see his

bare-naked white pasty ass. I'm Hella bothered now. He comes out of the bathroom trying to

argue with me about wanting to be on my bed. I told him "Get the fuck out of here leave the

kids alone. You can barely stand up and you're spilling alcohol on a 2-year-old". I'm getting

louder and louder. Will and Tyler come over and tell him to just go to the other room, but

Creep can't stop running his mouth. He starts talking crazy to Tyler and Will. Will tells him "It's

time for you to leave." Creep storms out. He goes to the front office. Pulls his deposit on the

room and says he wants to kick everyone out of "his room." Thankfully half of the room was

already paid for, and the reservation was in my name. So, Creep couldn't kick us out but what

a piece of shit for even trying. Tyler and Will go down to the front desk to pay and give creep his stuff. He tries to snatch it out of Will's hand but being sloppy drunk he ended up just dropping his own bag. It had his Nintendo switch in it. He accused Will of trying break his switch. He acted like he wanted to fight but could barely stand straight. Will said "dude you need to leave. Go sleep it off." Will is a big guy, he's six foot 5 and 200 pounds. Creep is a little turd five foot 6 and 160 pounds. Tyler being a nice guy offers to pay for Creep to have an Uber. Creep is texting me talking shit. I told Tyler to say fuck him and cancel the uber halfway through the drive since he wants to be a bitch, he can pay for his own uber. Tyler mid drive cancels Creeps uber. Becky said now she knew what kind of a person creep was and was done. This was just acid talking because she stayed on and off with creep for a month after this. Continuing to drink and sneak out. She at first lied to me about it because she knew I didn't like him or approve of her leading Tyler on and using him because it was cheating in my eyes. I'm not her mother but as a friend I would want my friend to hold me accountable to when I'm doing something fucked up. Becky eventually broke up with creep after she found out he was raw dogging the ex-who's house he was living in. She went through a depressive episode. I tried to be as supportive as I could. I always texted first. Asked her how she was.

Offered to go over to her house so she wouldn't have to travel. Reassured her it was normal

to be sad about a breakup. She distanced herself from me. I didn't take it personally at first

until she made some shady posts. I knew how that went. EVERY single fight our friendship had

went the same. She made shady posts. I asked her about it. She denied it was about me when

it clearly was. I got pissed off. I told her off. Then she made more posts about me. Anyways

back to the main storyline. One of our mutual friends said she had posted a TikTok from her

birthday. Remember the one I asked her not to post? It was deleted within 15 minutes. I didn't

even say anything, but I was pissed she posted it when I had asked her not to. Becky's fake

behavior was just getting more obvious. I started distancing myself. I would post my TikTok

drafts before texting her back. This made her mad. She got increasingly passive aggressive.

Posting more shady things. If I'd not texted her back for an hour, she'd wait two, if I waited

four, she'd wait eight. It was a petty mind game we were both playing. My Son's first birthday

was coming up. I had plans for a small gathering. I didn't want to do anything crazy because he was only one. I decided we'd go to the arcade. I rented a room for his birthday party. Set it

up cute. Got a big cake, balloons, the works. I am not afraid to blow money on my child. I got

game cards for all my party members. I'd invited Will's mom and dad, Paradise and her

boyfriend Row, Miles, his girlfriend Naya, Becky, and Tyler. The party started at 1. Becky was

late. She arrived at 1:45. She smelled like alcohol and weed. Everyone at the party knew she

was drunk. She then goes immediately to the bar and gets a drink. I tell her we are all going

bowling. Everything's paid for. Just tell them yours and Tyler's shoe size. Will's mom and Becky

go to order their shoes at the exact same time. Will's mom orders a size six. Becky orders a

size ten. Without thinking Will's 66-year-old mom says, "WOW big feet". She didn't mean for

what she said to sound like an insult, but Becky took it VERY personally. She started having a

tantrum. She pulled me aside at my sons 1 year old party to rant for 5 minutes about how

Will's mom was such a bitch for saying she had big feet. You do have big feet... the fuck. All I

thought of in that moment was how selfish she was. Pulling me aside to bitch about how she

doesn't have big feet when she does who the fuck cares. IT'S FEET. Late. Hungover. Terrible ass friend. When it was her son's birthday, I helped with everything, but this bitch couldn't even be on time or sober and HAD TO FIND SOMETHING TO MAKE HER THE CENTER OF ATTENTION. I told her I'm sure she didn't mean to be offensive. She's an extremely sweet lady. She just says whatever's on the top of her mind. Old people say shit. Becky after downing a second drink at the bar leaves. She wasn't even at my son's party for a half hour. I was extremely irritated and disappointed. Paradise and Miles didn't like Becky. Everyone at the party said she was rude and drunk. She made a complete ass of herself. She didn't even care. She ate up so much time causing drama taking me away from my son. After she left, we had a wonderful time. Eating cake, opened gifts, playing games, we even played laser tag. My son had an amazing first birthday. After 4 hours of playing games, bowling, pizza, laser tag and mini golfing we went home. My son was exhausted and fell asleep. After my son's party there was a lot of tension between Becky and me. I wasn't trying to hide it. I would purposely not respond. I started getting increased hate comments from fake accounts. One day I decided to try and login to one of the fake accounts. I entered the account that had left a personal comment and clicked forgot password. There were two options one was to send code to email the other was send code to phone number. I clicked send code to email first. The email was

her zodiac sign. I re-entered the username and clicked forgot password a second time. This

time I clicked the send code to phone number is showed the last four digits of her phone

number. Within minutes of me sending this confirmation text the account was deleted. Becky

dropped her attitude and started sending me funny memes and videos. Trying to deflect her

obvious guilt. I ignored her for 24 hours. Coming to terms and trying to decide what I should

do. I talked with my siblings. Paradise said I should beat her up or file a restraining order.

Miles said I should beat her up. Will said I should just block her and say nothing. I knew no

matter what I did it would go the same way it had every other time Becky and I fell out. Every

other time I'd fallen out with her the first thing she did was take to social media to trash my

name. In the past I had retaliated after. I didn't want to do that this time. I decided I needed

to be 100% sure. I had to find a way to prove it was her. A fake account linked to her phone

number is damning evidence, but she would just blame Tyler or say it was faked. I had to

prove it. Truthfully, I also didn't want to believe it. Pretending to be my stalker knowing how

traumatizing that was for me. This was all over her own insecurities. She started calling me over and over crying. I asked her "Why was your phone number linked to the TikTok account that leaked my address?" She played coy. She said she got a confirmation code but that she didn't know what it was for. I screen recorded on my phone. (I still have this screen recording). I always keep receipts of EVERYTHING. I entered in the fake account username. I clicked forgot password even though the fake account was already deleted or deactivated. I'm not sure how that works. I sent the confirmation to the number. She sent me back the code. I entered it. It logged me into her main TikTok account. I was disgusted. She had linked her phone number on the fake account, deleted the fake account and relinked it back to her normal account. She knew the day before when I had sent the confirmation code someone was trying to login to it. I hung up on her. She called me back crying and saying it wasn't her, someone must have done it. Bitch please, how did someone confirm a phone number on a TikTok account, and you just didn't know? She says she's going to the police station. I tell her yeah... you do that. Typical narcissist. Go to the police. Pretend to be a victim. I knew she was and I had to prove it. I decided that I would wait for the right time. Becky told me she was pregnant 2 days after this. She wasn't sure for a second time who the father was. She was

sure it was Tyler's but not 100%. She went on and on about how much this new baby would

do, nothing but cause problems. How she couldn't afford it, how postpartum depression

affected her and how much she hated herself and body after having a baby. She could not

financially provide for the baby. She wasn't in a stable relationship. She didn't have a job. She

didn't have nor could afford a house. She was purposely trying to get pregnant. Becky always

wanted attention. Good or bad. Calling me to vent about the pregnancy was just because she

wanted something to get attention about hoping to deflect my anger by making me feel like

she needed me. I wasn't happy for her because I knew what kind of a mother, she was to the

child she had. I felt bad for her son. He didn't deserve two parents who fought all the time.

Yelled at him. Hit him. I gave my honest opinion. I told her she should get an abortion. She at

first pretended to be offended then considered the option. Saying it would "be better but she

doesn't think she can go through with it." It wouldn't be an easy choice but it's an option you

have. I told her I supported her decision either way. Becky was having extreme morning

sickness. She was moody. She talked shit about her friend Anthony and Ember all the time.

She said Anthony was a loud alcoholic who only wanted to get high or turn up. Ember was

dirty and her daughter was bad. It wasn't even less than two weeks later Becky was back to

leaving nasty comments from fake TikTok accounts. I knew it was her, so I set her up. I left a

specific comment under my pregnancy video and took a screenshot of the exact time. The

comment was something ONLY she knew. Even if she had friends lurking, which she didn't.

They wouldn't know what I was talking about. The comment was about how I was miserable

when I was pregnant because someone who I had trusted leaked all my most personal secrets

causing me to be severely bullied. Within 10 minutes of me leaving this comment under my

video Becky blocked me through text message. I had already had her blocked on TikTok,

snapchat, and Instagram. She began making post after post on TikTok bashing me. I still have

the screen recordings. I knew it was her all along. I now had irrefutable evidence. The specific

hate comments, the copied videos, the phone number, the direct response to the comment. I

have forgiven her. However, I am DONE letting other people tell my life story. You don't get to

say how I reacted was wrong when you don't tell the parts of what you did to get that

reaction. I don't start shit, I finish it.

CHAPTER 11

BLOSSOMING.

When I first started TikTok I made meaningless thirst traps. I had no idea what to post. I

decided I wanted to pursue something I never thought I could do. I wanted to be a makeup

artist. I wanted to tell true crime. Somewhere down the line the way I was doing it wasn't the

most respectful, so I changed the way I told my stories. Eventually I completely stopped

posting true crime stories that either didn't have a happy conclusion or had somebody who

was still currently needing help. Petitions, most wanted, people with go fund Me's. If it wasn't

helping someone or bringing active awareness it wasn't something I wanted to post about. On

Mother's Day of 2020 I posted my very first personal life story. I didn't think it would go viral. I

didn't care about it going viral. I just wanted to vent about something awful my mother had

done. It blew up. From then on, I continued opening about my horrific childhood. I got more

traction. Millions of views, thousands of comments, hundreds of likes. I found an entire

community of people who not only supported me, but many had gone through a lot of similar

things. I had become a beacon of hope for people struggling with things I had overcome. I was

proof that even after years of sexual, physical, and verbal abuse you could do something with your life. You'd make it out. You can cut all those people off. You can start with nothing and work into something. You can hone one or many talents. You can have everything you dreamed of. It won't be an easy route but it's never impossible. I began getting back into art. Drawings, paintings, sculptures. I pursued a new career path. I paid $19,000 out of pocket and got my messed-up teeth fixed. I Learned and tried so many new things. Crocheting, sewing, knitting, I went Kayaking, paddle boarding, river rafting, tubing, swimming, rode rollercoasters, went skydiving, roller skating, roller blading, skateboarding, made tons of DIY crafts and home goods. I bought two cars and my first house. I took a shower for the first time in years after being traumatized by my grandfather. Baths are no longer my only option. I struggled with my weight and recovering from an eating disorder. I hired a nutritionist to aid me with my diet. I joined a gym. I've done martial arts, Yoga, Pilates and gone to the gym consistently for an entire year. I have not missed a single day. I lost one hundred pounds. I'm the strongest and healthiest I've ever been. I'm the most talented I've ever been. I'm the best version of myself I have ever been. Every hardship I've endured has led me up to this point in my life where I've found happiness and peace. I have a beautiful family. I don't have a mom or a dad. I have a brother and a sister. I have a partner. I have an amazing son. My family may be little but its so meaningful. It's the family I chose. I want to thank everyone for reading my life. Thank you for your kindness, support and listening ears. Starting to tell my story has brought me great peace, satisfaction and given me my power back. I felt alone for the longest. I never spoke about the things that happened to me. I let other people tell my life story for their own entertainment. When I was a little girl, I used to draft stories in a notebook. Stories where a hero would save the struggling girl. I hope that I am someone's hero. I hope that someone reading this has a different reflection on life. Someday things will get better. You can overcome any trauma or obstacles. I know it sounds dumb and cliché. You don't have to be born into money or power to have it. I hoped as a child that someday I'd grow up to be someone meaningful. Someone who would change lives. Thank you for being here. There will be a second book. I still have so many secrets I don't want to keep.

Made in the USA
Monee, IL
30 August 2023

41890487R00103